SUCCESS FUNDAS

Success Fundas
By J K Nair

Self Help/ Motivation
English Language

Published by:
Max books
Maxlive Media Solutions Pvt Ltd.
Muppathiyil Building, Muttambalom Post,
Kanjikuzhy, Kottayam 686 004
maxlivemediasolutions@gmail.com
Ph: 90740 98776, 73060 23373
Online Bookstore :
wwwmaxbooksonline.com

Printed in India
at Penta Offset, Kottayam

Edition:
First Edition 2021

Price : Rs. 199/-

ISBN
978-93-91085-08-7

SUCCESS FUNDAS

J K NAIR
International Motivator,
Softskill Trainer and Educator

MaX BOOKS

ABOUT THE AUTHOR

A very Confident, Inspiring, and Dynamic Personality, Mr. J K Nair is not a new face in the corporate world. **WE CANNOT SPELL S_CCESS WITHOUT YOU** - that is the gospel of Soft Skill Trainer, Author, Educator and International Ace Motivator Mr. J K Nair. He believes that for the success of any individual, other people play a very VITAL role. He is the founder of M/s. Vital Training, a training institution of repute. A much sought after speaker and a successful person, JK has many feathers in his cap. With 23+ years of experience in Training and HR, he has given training to 3,00,000+ staffs of various 200 plus corporate companies, schools, colleges and institutions. He has written his maiden book on "Success is not anybody's Monopoly" in the year 2013 basically on success principles. He has also written a book titled "Developing Leadership Muscles"

By Qualification he is B.Com, LLB, Post Graduate Diploma in Industrial Relation and Personnel Management. He is a Member of Ahmedabad Management Association-Ahmedabad, Hon. Secretary of National Institute of Personnel Management (NIPM)-Surat Chapter, Vadodara Chamber of Commerce and Industry, Vadodara-Gujarat, Bharuch District Management Association, Bharuch-Gujarat etc.

He is a voracious reader and having more than 1700 books in his personal library. He is a community leader involving in much community social work and was the President of Federation of Gujarat Malayalee Association for 4 years, an apex body of all Malayalee Associations in Gujarat, covering approximately 10 lakhs of Malayalees.

He is also an acclaimed Columnist & has written several magazine articles for a prominent publication. He has also appeared in Television Interviews to promote education & soft skill training. He has also acted in Malayalam film.

- He has won **"National Achievers"** Award for Excellence in HRD for his contribution in the field of Training and HRD from Indian Economic Development and Research Association (IERDA), New Delhi for the year 2012.
- He has also won another prestigious award **"Mother Teresa Excellence Award"** for Educational Training Services. Instituted by Integrated Council for Socio-Economic Progress. Trichur-Kerala which was awarded to him on 23rd June. 2013 at Hyderabad.
- In 2014 January he won one more prestigious award on **"Innovative Trainer Award"** from Indian Society for Training and Development (lSTD), Vadodara-Gujarat, a premier and pioneer training and development institute in India.
- In 2014 he has also won award **"School Of Educators Global Education"** from New Delhi for outstanding contribution to Innovation and Technology in Training.
- In 2016. He has won **"Innovation in Educator"** Award 2016 from CKSVIM-Vadodara, Gujarat.
- He has attended National HR Conference–of IPM SriLanka in June 2017 as Indian Delegate of NIPM-India.

ACKNOWLEDGEMENT

Writing of this maiden book has taken many years of my reading, teaching and experience with participants. Many people have contributed to my thinking and have been invisible guides as the chapters developed together.

First of all, I thank my wonderful wife Indira for believing and supporting me always to do greater things. Her love and affection has been a source of inspiration. She always stood beside me when I had to take tough decisions in life.

My special thanks to my fabulous and incredible son Vivek for being very positive towards me, for his invaluable inputs and constant support. He amazed me with his wisdom, insight and talents. He is a trouble shooter for me, whenever I stuck with some problems; he is always there besides me to assist. I am very proud of you my son.

I am thankful to my parents, relatives, friends for supporting in my every endeavour and also express my thanks to all my critics, who directly or indirectly a source of great inspiration for me.

I would be failing my duty, if I do not acknowledge the contribution of all participants across India and abroad from corporate, schools, colleges and institutions who have attended my various seminars and training. Their constant support and follow-up have inspired me to complete the book.

I am thankful to my Ex-employer Krishak Bharati Cooperative Limited (KRIBHCO), Surat; such a great company to work with. I would not be who I am without the freedom that management has given to me during my 24 years of service. And while I was working in this great organisation, I developed myself as a soft skill trainer, but could not get a chance to conduct a training programme for the employees of this organisation. However, since last 4 years I am regularly conducting training programme for my friends in Kribhco, which I feel is a great success for me. My special thanks to Top Management, HR and Training Department, Union, Association and all my friends in Kribhco.

I am thankful to many great authors and speakers whose writings and audio-videos helped me in shaping my life. I am also thankful to all those who directly or indirectly helped me in fulfilling my dreams.

J K Nair

CONTENTS

PREFACE

There is a substantial portion of the world population that believes that success is a birthright, that it's something written or fated to happen to only select few people. Nothing could be farther from the truth. Success is not the destiny of a few. Success is not anybody's monopoly. Success is achieved not by design, but by desire. A driving force inside you is what helps one achieve success.

Success is a process, it's a journey, an arduous, grueling and taxing albeit rewarding journey. This journey can be rewarding but it's not going to be easy. And the road to success is not reserved only for the few, but it is open to the many. But only few have the courage, strength, perseverance and integrity to follow through. You too can achieve success if you have the right mentality and the required tools, which can be inculcated within yourself.

Your success is contingent on both internal and external factors. The external factors are your surroundings and environment, things which you have no control upon. They may be harmful or helpful. Either way, it is not something that you can decide for yourself, it is usually thrust upon you. Now the internal factors that your success depends upon are completely in your control. These internal factors are what govern your chances of success.

There are several such factors that are discussed in this book. These will provide insight into your mind and it's workings. How your mentality can alter your mindset, and how an altered mindset can lead to a greater and brighter future.

One of those factors that can get you to the doorway of success is 'Dreams'. It is the very existence of dreams, goals and desires that helps a person get up and get going everyday towards it. There are several other factors such as Happiness, Goals, Habits, Self-Esteem and Personality. Each of these traits is key factors that can help you become whoever you want to be.

Human beings have unlimited power hidden within themselves, which they do not know about. You too have the same power hidden within. When you start working towards achieving your dreams, when you focus on what you want and do everything you can do get to where you want to go, then you can unlock this deep power and harness it to become a successful person.

INTRODUCTION

Have you ever wondered why one person is happy and the other is sad? Why one person is a great success and other an absolute failure? Why one person is rich and prosperous and the other is poor and miserable? Why one person is having happy married life and the other is having a totally ruined family?

You might have come across many people who always roam here and there without any work, expecting the fortune to kiss them every time and everywhere. They are the one who suffer the entire life due to frustration and unhappiness. But I am sure you are not one amongst them, the very simple fact that you have picked up this book at the right time. You have a desire to **update, uplift and upgrade** your life and that desire has now turned into a decision. Yes, you have now taken an **"Appointment With Your Future"**. This book will lead you from darkness to light and will make you an extra ordinary person.

For most of us, life should be pretty good. Just imagine - professional success, happiness, good health, reasonably prosperous, secure, good friends, social status, peace, sound financial security, good family relationships and many good things in our life. You can achieve all these and many more, provided you walk a few miles with me and I guarantee **'there will be no looking back'**. You are heading for attaining happiness and success irrespective of who you are, what you are, where you are, what education you have and how much wealth you have.

This is a book of great principles with powerful motivational tips used by successful people all over the world. This book will change your life. I give absolute guarantee of success in your life. When you finish reading, you will say, yes this is one of the best readings I had in my life. By having a healthy calories food, you won't put up weight, you have to eat continuously. Likewise, by reading this book once you cannot expect to bring transformation in your life.

Read it, re-read it and make it as an important guide of your life. What you have to do is to apply the learning in your life. You don't need to bring changes 100% in one area of your life and that is not easily possible also. However, you can bring 1% improvement in 100 areas and over a period of time, 100% changes will come in your life. Make small changes and that will change everything in your life.

I have extensively studied these success principles over 23 years and have applied them in my personal and professional life. The level of success I enjoy is the outcome of implementing them since I began imparting training programmes and I feel privileged to have the opportunity to share the power packed proven principles of success to you.

The strategies, principles, tools and techniques written in this book will always work if you work on them. Anyone can repeatedly produce the kind of results they want. **All you have to do is to decide what you want, believe you deserve it and practice the success principles.**

SUCCESS IS NOT ANYBODY'S MONOPOLY:

Everyone can achieve success, it doesn't matter whether you are unemployed, illiterate, or having a low profile job. All you have to do is to learn these tools, practice them and put them to use in your favour. Witness the miracles that are going to happen. I am going to give you a road map, you can decide where you want to go, take the help of the road map and proceed to your goal.

Your life is like a combination lock; to open the lock you need to find the right numbers in the right order, and then it is going to open for you whether you are poor, rich, a salesman, an actor, a clerk or a high profile businessman. Inversely if you do not put anything inside the bag, you cannot take anything out of it. Similarly in life too, the more you put in, the more you can draw out.

Everything that you are going to read from here is based on various techniques, principles and ways aimed towards success. At the end of this reading, you can choose your own unique way to achieve success. Why is it so? It's because, as a unique human being the definition of success differs for everyone. No one has ever defined or quantified success such that it is applicable to everyone. It changes from person to person. One thing I can assure you is that the techniques and principles that I am going to explore here will transform you as a person and bring you back into the flow of success that is already waiting for you at your door step.

You are all on board to take a journey with me to success that is going to bring you all back into the stream of a happy and fulfilled life. Fasten your seat belts. It's now time to take off on a journey that will profoundly change your life. If you are ready, let us start a very special journey towards dominating success, health, wealth and happiness.

From here, let us stop or at least the begin the end of all negative thinking, believing, behaviour, reaction, of being influenced by negative people and settling for less than what you deserve. That is the commitment that you need to make right now.

GROUND RULES FOR THE GAME OF LIFE

The basic purpose of writing this book is to help you to ***"change yourself in the best possible way by finding out yourself"*.**

For a while, consider me as a coach and yourself as my player. Being a player, you have to follow some ground rules, before playing the game. These rules are equally important in the game of life too.

PARTICIPATE:

The first rule is PARTICIPATION. Your life is divided into two parts; **one is the family life and the other is the professional life.** You spend almost the same time at both the places. Usually most of us can run our affairs correctly in one place, but are unable manage the other, which creates an imbalance in our life. The tension and stress generated in one place is automatically carried to other. Therefore, you are unable to participate fully in any activities at either place. There must be a holistic approach. You are not an arm and a leg, but a complete human being. The whole person goes to work and the whole person comes home. You take your family problems to work and work problems to your home. There is always an import-export of tension from work to home and home to work. Then what happens? Your stress level goes up and productivity comes down. The whole person is employed at the job, not just a part of you. And the salary is paid for the whole person.

There are two types of people in this world:

One is **TGIM** and the other is **OGIM**. The TGIM people are highly energetic, excited, passionate, confident, courageous, humorous, cheerful and enthusiastic. Wherever they go, whether it is workplace, in community services or in the family, they carry these highly inflammable emotions with them. They are passionate enough to do anything. They are crazy.

Crazy people make history;
other people read history

The OGIM people simply drag their feet; they lack the above mentioned emotions. They lack enthusiasm, energy and excitement. Can you crack what is TGIM and OGIM?

TGIM means - **'Thanks God It's Monday'**, and OGIM means **'Oh God It's Monday'**. There is a lot difference in attitude between the two. The person with TGIM quality will be the best option for an organization. However, most people carry the OGIM feeling. They come to work, but don't have the right kind of mood. In today's world, corporate is not worried about absenteeism. If one person is absent, somebody else can take over. But the biggest problem is presenteeism, implying that after they come to work, they just pull on. There exists a mentality of two punches and one lunch. Some people make things happen; some people watch things happen and others wonder what happened.

When I get up in the morning, at 4.00 AM what do I do – first of all I thank God that I am alive in this world. And as soon as I put my feet down, I say with power and conviction, the following powerful affirmations with the right emotions:

- It's going to be a great day.
- I am the best
- I can do it
- God is always with me
- I can handle more than I think I can

- There is always something to be happy about
- I am going to make someone happy today
- Life is great, make the most of it.
- I am a winner
- Today is my day

With these auto-suggestions or affirmations, I become so positive and I feel that I am ready to do something. Emotions like passion, energy, excitement, enthusiastic, sense of humour, fire in the belly, cheerfulness, self-confidence will not be produced automatically. You need to produce these emotions deliberately, regularly and unnaturally for some days, till it imprints in your subconscious mind. To cultivate a rose garden, you need to work a lot, however, for wild weeds to appear, you don't have to do anything. Similarly to have a positive frame of mind, you need to work hard. Negativity is like a weed, it will grow automatically. How you get up in the morning will play a big part in how high you go up in life.

How you greet people and observe manners, etiquettes, gestures, postures, body language, way of dressing, sitting, walking, using fingers, actions, smiling, laughing, shaking hands; these all indicate how energetic you are; how enthusiastic you are; how excited you are; how confident and courageous you are.

Your face is like a mirror. It is a moving autobiography. Several communication experts say that your face can make 7000 expressions. A simple smile, a firm shake-hand, a kind word and a gentle hug - that is more than enough to include the other person on your side.

Do you know how many times a small baby since its birth either smiles or laughs on an average in a day? Approximately 450 to 500 times in a day! Even in sleep they smile. And what about us – adults like you and me? Only 10 to 15 times a day - which means we used to laugh a lot when we were children. But slowly the number has been reduced to bare minimum.

We used to laugh to forget but we have forgotten to laugh. So keep smiling and activate all your systems. A smile takes only 12 muscles of your face, whereas when you frown, you use 72 muscles. Can you smile and be angry at the same time? Anger is one letter short of Danger. Anger is the biggest enemy of human health. Conquer your anger and conquer hour health. Whereas other side smile always dominates. A smile costs nothing, but gives many returns; it enriches those who receive it, without making those who give it poorer for it. It takes a moment, but the memory of it sometimes lasts forever. It increases your face value.

Smiling is a cooling system of the heart, sparkling system of the eyes, lightening system of the face, and relaxing system of the mind.

When I say participation, it means to physically stay and mentally "**be**" in the activity you are doing. If you are playing cricket, play cricket, don't think about the people in the pavilion; otherwise you will be in the pavilion soon. While reading this book, you may slip out frequently for brief trips to some other jobs; say for example preparing for a picnic, watching a cricket match, teaching your kids, etc. It is injustice to the work you do. Active participation makes any work interesting and lively.

It's not "when you are alive you participate". It's "when you participate you are alive".

After the 2nd world war, America had enough money. Immediately there wasn't going to be any wars then. So they decided to invest the money into some businesses. They had money, education and infrastructure, but they did not have sufficient manpower to do jobs. So they asked people from all over the world to come with their **HANDS**. We will use our heads. People started working for America, they just used their hands and not brains. So there was stability in the business, even though the progress was slow. America would use its authority to rule and pass instructions downward for meeting its targets. It was a type of military system, an autocratic style of functioning, where ruling and operations were like a pyramid. Orders would be issued from the top and others would just have to follow. This system worked for almost 30 years.

After 30 years, Japan emerged in the business scenario. They adopted a society-based culture and Americans liked an individual based culture. Japan said, you are coming anyhow, why come with just your hands, bring your **HEAD** along. Here head meant thinking, giving suggestions and ideas, using intelligence, creativity, etc. So the people then started to use their head in the business, which brought quality products into the market. Japan invited their employees for their suggestions, opinions and creativity in the business. They believed in total quality management.

However, too many heads working together created lot of problems in management. What are the problems likely to occur when people work together? Ego clashes, differences of opinion, lack of trust, boss-subordinate relationship problems, lack of communication, no team work, nobody wants to take leadership, responsibility, etc. Organizations wanted their employees to produce more.

Then the world thought of bringing something more into the business i.e. adding the **HEART** or soul into the business. Hand and head training is done in schools and colleges but heart training isn't done anywhere. If you have hand and head but no heart in the job, it is a waste. If you have heart in the job, automatically the hand and head will get working. In other way, **Hand, head and heart means skill, knowledge and attitude respectively.**

Therefore, wherever you go, whatever you do, carry your HAND, HEAD and HEART into the job. How can you take heart into your business?

Here heart means:

1. Responsibility
2. Commitment
3. Motivation
4. Listening
5. Enthusiasm
6. Sense of Ownership

Put your job into your HEART and your Heart into the JOB

1. RESPONSIBILITY:

Responsibility is simply the ability to respond at any time and to any situation in a way that honours you as a person and supports you in your relationships with others. Contrast this with how we have been trained to view responsibility. People with character accept responsibilities. They make decisions and determine their own destiny in life. Accepting responsibilities involves taking risks and being accountable which is sometimes uncomfortable.

Responsibility does not involve blame, fault, or burden. Not being responsible does not connote shame, guilt or unworthiness. It does not involve a value judgment subject to someone's opinion about how you "should" do something or how someone ought to run their life. Responsibility instead involves taking full acceptance for every event, relationship, action and situation that occurs in your life.

People are ready to work, but when it comes to bear the responsibility, they withdraw themselves. They push others to the front to take responsibility. Proactive people always take responsibility. They are value driven. Proactive people are leaders whereas reactive people are followers.

Responsibility means, the "Ability to Respond"

As far as taking responsibility is concerned, what a good person says;

If anything goes really bad, I did it.
If anything goes semi-good, then we did it.
If anything goes really good, they did it.

That is all it takes to get people to win. In a corporate HR head office I have noticed a board meant for the customers, in which it was written that, if you are satisfied with the behaviour or services of any of our employees, go and congratulate them because they have done it. If you are not satisfied, then come and tell me; I take complete responsibility for their misbehaviour or poor performance.

Taking responsibility means
giving up your right to make others wrong.

Take 100% responsibility of your life; means you agree that whatever happened to you as on date and whatever is going to happen in your life, whether it is good or bad, positive or negative, more or less, you are responsible. If you have created something in your life, you can un-create the unwanted situations and re-create the desired outcomes. Once you realize that you are the reason for what happens in your life, it is easy to identify yourself and create whatever you want.

Therefore, you must take personal responsibility on your shoulder. You cannot throw the responsibility on other's shoulders. If something is done right, do you take the credit and if something goes wrong, do you throw it on others? You cannot change the situations, the seasons, or the wind, but you can always change yourselves.

Normally, lots of people have a mentality that they are entitled to everything in life. Someone, somehow, somewhere is responsible for satisfying their lives with continuous happiness, exciting advancement of career, etc. simply because they are born. But you know the fact is that there is only one person responsible for the quality of the life you live and that **person is you**. No one else is responsible for your life! Most people would rather stay in their comfort zone and live passive lives without accepting responsibilities. They drift through life waiting for things to happen rather than making them happen.

Responsible people don't think that the world owes them a living.

If you want to be successful, first of all take full responsibility for everything that you experience in your life whether it is about the results you produce, the relationships you have, your income, the condition of your health, your education, your feelings, your emotions, anything and everything.

ARE YOU IN A COMPLAINING AND BLAMING COUNTER?

If you want to be really successful, you will have to give up all the complaining and blaming and take total responsibility for your life. If you realize that you have created your current conditions; then you can un-create them and re-create them at will. So at first stage, realize that the entire responsibility of success and failure in your life lies upon you.

Unconditionally give up all blaming and excuses, all reasons of your failures, why you can't and why you haven't up until now, and all your blaming of outside situations or events.

In everyday life, we normally say to our children – listen, I have told you a hundred times to not watch cartoons, not play with mobile; or you have told your wife a hundred times not to prepare that particular vegetable; several times you requested your superiors, this is not the right way; you have instructed your subordinates so many times. Hundreds of times you tell them not to do such and such things; and still you haven't produced the results, then how can you expect new and different results at the hundred and first time, **that is nothing but insane.**

The definition of insanity is

"Doing the same thing over and over and expecting different results".

Now who is insane, your child, wife, superior, subordinate or you? Of course it's YOU. You expect change from your wife; son, boss, subordinate and entire world, but you don't want to change.

If you keep on telling them what you have always been telling them, you will keep on getting what you have always been getting. Continuing the same behaviour and expecting a different result is really insanity. If you continue your current behaviour, your life is not going to get any better.

Response
↑
Events ⟵ **E + R / R = R** ⟶ Results
↓
Reaction

EVENT + RESPONSE / REACTION = RESULTS

Look at the above formula **E + R / R = R** – The last "**R**" is **RESULTS.** This formula will work for you, if it is put into practice. Formula doesn't care who applies, if you apply it properly it will produce results. Formula doesn't play politics, it applies to all. It doesn't make choices. It has no preferences. Gravity will work the same way to everybody. Like that every principle, formula or science doesn't play favouritism; it is equal to all, provided you work on the principles. Science believes what works for one if experimented properly and applied properly it will work for everybody. If you combine two atoms of hydrogen and one atom of oxygen, you will get water, not sometimes, but always and everywhere. If you combine one atom of carbon and one atom of oxygen, it will be carbon monoxide, which is a poisonous gas. If you add one more atom of oxygen, it will be carbon dioxide, which is vital to plant and harmless to animals. A piece of steel expands when it is heated, whether the steel is manufactured in India, America or Japan. So it is very important to work on the above formula.

First of all you must think and decide what Results you want in your life? You all are working to achieve some results in life. You joined your organisation, because you want money, progress, better career etc; you joined a particular college, because you want to get a degree; you got married, because you need a partner to take care of each other. Whatever you do is to get some results.

Now "**E**" means **EVENTS**, or circumstances. Every day you come across several events in your life. There may be a few challenges, problems at home, at office or at any other place. If you have already told someone to do some work a hundred times and still they haven't done it, then there is no point in telling them the hundred and first time. After asking them two or three times, you should have understood that there is something wrong with your dialogue. You could have changed your **RESPONSE** (the other "R"), the approach or the way you ask them to do the job. You could have changed the way you **RESPOND**, as you have not produced the results. But what you normally do is "**REACT**". You react to every situation if the desired results are not produced. And a reaction is negative whereas a response is positive.

If you observe almost all the results you have gotten in your life, whether it is good or bad, more or less, positive or negative, in regards to success or failure, wealth or poverty, health or illness, happiness or unhappiness, it is because of how you have either Responded or Reacted to earlier Events or situations in your life. You always complain about your lack of results over any event. You have little or no control on the event; it is external, like the words of others, a situation beyond your reach.

You cannot go on blaming and complaining the outside world for the lack of results you are getting. It is because of either your response or your reaction to that particular event.

All blame is a waste of time.

No matter how much fault you find in others and regardless of how much you blame others, it will not change you. Everyone is producing results every time. Failure is also a result. But are you getting the **DESIRED RESULTS?**

Most of your failure or success comes from your habit of making excuses. You will have either excuses or good results – not both.

If you dislike the outcomes you are currently getting, you have got two choices - one is to complain or blame the event for your lack of results. That is what most people do, because it is easy to blame and complain others. You can blame the government, economy, poor facilities, your wife or husband, your boss's attitude, your parents, your children and so on. No doubt, all these factors exist, but if they were the deciding factor, nobody would ever succeed. Under these events and circumstances, how are others succeeding?

If you are not happy with your superior, you go and complain to your wife; if you are not happy with your wife, you go and complain to your friends! You are always complaining to the wrong people. Why do you do that? Because it provides some relief, nobody is there to listen you and also because there is no risk in that. **If you want to produce the desired results in life, complaint to the right person.** Right complaint to right counter produces results.

Secondly what you can do is to change your response to the event. The day you change your response is the day your life will begin to get better. If you want something different, you are going to have to do something different. **Same actions produce same results; different actions produce different results; extra actions produce extra results.** When your child or wife don't behave the way you want them to, you start reacting rather than changing your response or approach to the event. Reaction is negative and response is positive. When the medicine is reacting, it is negative, but when the medicine is responding, it is positive. Go on changing your response or approach to the particular event or situations till you get the result that you want.

Many people overcome so-called limiting factors, so it can't be the limiting factors that restrain us. It is not the external events, conditions and circumstances that limit you, it is only you. You stop yourselves from action or inaction. You normally have a habit of having limiting thoughts and engaging in self-defeating and unwanted behaviour. You defend your own habits which are not taking you towards your goals, such as over sleeping, gossiping, irrelevant watching of TV, smoking, chewing tobacco and drinking alcohol justified by some logics which are indefensible. You bypass, ignore, reject or neglect useful feedback; you fail to continuously educate yourselves, learn to add new skills, waste your time on unwanted things of our lives, engage in gossiping, eat junk food, fail to exercise, spend more money than you make, don't ask for what you want, and then wonder why things don't work out. This is what most people do. They blame the outside events and circumstances.

People have an excuse for everything.

You can change your response to every event, the way things are, until you get the results you want. You can change your thinking, change your behaviour, your communication, change the pictures you hold in your head, your images of yourself and the world, you can change the things the way you do. You really do have control on all of those. You are run by your habits that you never change. You get stuck in your conditioned response.

- In life, you have control over only three things -
the thoughts you think,
the images you visualize,
and the actions you take.

How you use these three things determines everything in your life. If you don't like the results you are producing, you need to work on your response and change it accordingly. Change your negative thoughts to positive. Change your bad habits to good habits. Change your job. Change what you read. Change your friends. Change how you talk. Change your environment.

If you want to get what you want from your life, of course you are going to have to take that risk. Learn to replace complaining with making requests and taking actions that will achieve your desired outcomes. If you find yourself in a situation you don't like, either work on it to make it better or leave. Don't just sit there and complain, do something. If you don't like the system, take initiative, be an activist and change or else simply leave it.

Whatever happens in your life is because of your action, inaction or reaction. All these results are invited by you because you simply did not act, or reacted. You have either created or allowed everything that happens to you. You used to get some warnings or alarm, either external or internal, in your life through your intuition, comments from others or may be the body language of other people or may be through your subconscious mind.

When you had chest pain and the doctor suggested an hours walk in the morning and evening, you ignored it; when you came home late every day and could not spend time with your wife and children and they showed their frustration and unhappiness through their body language, you ignored it; you developed a series of bad habits like drinking alcohol, smoking and your body started reacting, you ignored that too. You ignored all these useful warnings because paying attention to them would require you to do something that is uncomfortable.

Sometimes you feel that whatever you do is right. It isn't necessary that you are. You may be wrong. But if you take feedback from people, you can change yourselves for making your life better. Have you ever taken feedback from your boss about your performance, from your parents about your attitude? No. Taking feedback from others is the best method to keep improving. If they give negative feedback, treat it as a stepping stone towards success. You can work on your behaviour and display a new set of behaviour based on the feedback.

It is not even necessary to ask for feedback, you can always understand from their body language, their tone, use of words; the way they communicate to you. When you are late, your boss looks at the watch; it is a feedback. He does not say anything, but it indicates that you are late. When you had a quarrel with your children, they went inside their rooms and started crying. It is a feedback; it shows that they are unhappy with you. When your customer rejected the goods sent by you, it is a feedback. However, you have ignored these useful feedbacks and when the unwanted results come, you blame them. You are completely responsible for the results produced. You could have understood their body language and done things right sooner. But you won't take responsibility.

STORY:

One day a husband had a doubt that his wife that couldn't hear so well. So he went to the doctor and complained that his wife couldn't hear and he didn't know from what distance she could hear him. Is there any test to identify the distance from how far she can hear? Doctor said, its simple, first you ask her something from a distance of five metres and if she doesn't respond, it means she can't hear from that distance, then repeat the same from four metres, three metres, two metres and one meter. So do that and then come and tell me the result, so that I can start the treatment.

So he went home and asked his wife from a distance of five metres, while she was working in kitchen. "Hello dear, is the food ready?" There was no response from her, so he moved to four metres distance and repeated the same question, again no response. He repeated this until he was only a meter away. But again there was no response. So he stood very close to her and asked, "Hello dear, Is the food ready?" Then finally she said, I have already told you five times that the food is ready. If you can't hear me then what can I do?" So the fault was not with her but in him. However, he threw the blame on others. Similarly, there will be instances when you won't take responsibility. Therefore, from today take 100% responsibility of your life. **You can't always blame the mirror for how you look.**

Always remember –
there is a way and that way is on the way.

WHAT IS THE OPPOSITE OF 'IMPORTANT'?

It is unimportant, irrelevant, inessential etc.; grammatically it is absolutely right. Let me ask you a question. Is it IMPORTANT to keep your boss happy or DIFFICULT to keep your boss happy? Is it important to spend time with your family or difficult? Is it important to study further or difficult? Is it important to save money or difficult? Is it important to keep yourself fit and energetic or difficult?

The moment you say it is difficult, you put a full stop. Now you will find many reasons and excuses to justify what you said are right. So the moment you say it is difficult to spend quality time with your family, you will find lots of excuses to show that whatever you said is right. Reverse the same – say to yourself, it is very important to spend quality time with your family. Now this is a question mark; you will ask yourself how and when I can spend time? It becomes a challenge. Now you will find time somehow, because again you want to justify what you said is right.

Therefore, the opposite word of IMPORTANT is DIFFICULT.

Whenever you have any problem, ask yourself, is it important or difficult. You will get the right answer and you won't find any excuses. Full stop is a death and a question mark is life.

Let us change from today – Now onwards, first of all YOU will think what RESULTS you want in your life in every situation. Make a list of results you want to get in your life. Once that is clear, you can change your Response or Approach towards the Event. Now after couple of approaches or few more deliberations, if you have not achieved the desired results; you change your approach till you get the results you want. And that is truly in your hands. You have not given this power to anyone. But you need to change yourselves and change your approach.

The important thing to remember is that, others are getting results in the same situation, within the same conditions. Why don't you get results? It means, there is something wrong with your response. Ask those who have produced better results in the same situation. They have a recipe for success. They can tell you how they produced results when they had faced the similar situations.

If you don't like your results, change your responses

WHAT IS THE MEANING OF POWER?

It is the ability to produce Results. And you have that ability and capability to produce the desired results. Since others are producing these results, then why can't you? Others are attaining success, then why can't you? The only thing you have to change is your response or approach towards the event till you get the DESIRED OUTCOME you want; keep on changing your approach. Power is making something happen without the use of force, not even appropriate force.

You may not be responsible for being knocked down, but you are responsible for getting back up

A classic example of taking Responsibility – narrated by late Hon'ble President of India Dr. APJ Abdul Kalam:

Kalam: Let me tell you about my experience. In 1973 I became the project director of India's satellite launch vehicle program, commonly called the SLV-3. Our goal was to put India's 'Rohini' satellite into orbit by 1980. I was given funds and human resources - but was told clearly that by 1980 we had to launch the satellite into space. Thousands of people worked together in scientific and technical teams towards that goal. By 1979 we thought we were ready. As the project director, I went to the control centre for the launch.

At four minutes before the satellite launch, the computer began to go through the checklist of items that needed to be checked. One minute later, the computer program put the launch on hold; the display showed that some control components were not in order. My experts - I had four of them with me - told me not to worry; they had done their calculations and there was enough reserve fuel. So I bypassed the computer, switched to manual mode, and launched the rocket. In the first stage, everything worked fine. In the second stage, a problem developed. Instead of the satellite going into orbit, the whole rocket system plunged into the Bay of Bengal . It was a big failure. That day, the Chairman of the Indian Space Research Organization, Prof. Satish Dhawan, had called a press conference. The launch was at 7:00 am, and the press conference, where journalists from around the world were present.

It was at 7:45 am at ISRO's satellite launch range in Sriharikota [in Andhra Pradesh in southern India]. Prof. Satish Dhawan, the leader of the organization, conducted the press conference himself. He took responsibility for the failure - he said that the team had worked very hard, but that it needed more technological support. He assured the media that in another year, the team would definitely succeed. Now, I was the project director, and it was my failure, but instead, he took responsibility for the failure as chairman of the organization. The next year, in July 1980, we tried again to launch the satellite - and this time we succeeded. The whole nation was jubilant. Again, there was a press conference. Prof. Satish

Dhawan called me aside and told me, 'You conduct the press conference today.' I learned a very important lesson that day. When failure occurred, the leader of the organization owned that failure. When success came, he gave it to his team. The best management lesson I have learned did not come to me from reading a book; it came from that experience.

Everything we experience today is the result of either our responses or reactions to the choices we have made in the past.

2. COMMITMENT:

The second meaning of HEART is commitment. Nobody wants to commit to anything because they have no confidence that they can fulfil their commitment. What is Commitment? Is it a Promise? Commitment means honouring your Word. Honouring your word means a commitment and not a mere promise. Think before uttering the word, but once you have given a word, keep it at any cost. Integrity and wisdom are the two pillars on which to build and keep commitments.

What is the difference between a Promise and a Commitment? Suppose you tell someone, I will get to your place in 10 minutes. Now at what time do you actually reach? In 15 minutes, 20 minutes; this would be a promise. But commitment means getting there in exactly 10 minutes. **Promise MAY be fulfilled, but Commitment WILL be fulfilled, SHALL be fulfilled, OUGHT to be fulfilled, MUST be fulfilled, HAVE to be fulfilled.** A promise is a statement of intent. A commitment is a promise that is going to be kept at all cost. Commitment comes out of character and leads to conviction. Uncommitted relationships are pretty shallow and hollow. They are matter of convenience and are temporary. The moment you commit and quit holding back, many unforeseen incidents, meetings and material assistance will rise up and support you. The very act of commitment is a powerful magnet for help.

To shoulder more responsibility plus honouring your word is the art of success.

Commitment is doing or not doing something (willingly – out of total freedom) in spite of the odds (unforeseen obstacles); means keeping your word despite of unforeseen circumstances, conditions or events.

It implies giving a word. When you give your word to someone, you give your word only. When you consistently give and fulfil your word, you become **Trustworthy**. When you are consistently trustworthy, you become a **Reliable** person. And when you are consistently reliable, become **Dependable**. When you are consistently dependable you will be **Useful** to the world. When you are consistently useful, you will be **Wanted** by all. When you are consistently wanted, you will be in great **Demand**. When you consistently in Demand, your **Position** will be top of the world. When you are consistently in great Position, you can **Negotiate** better. When you can consistently negotiate better, you Earn **Profits** and Give more value based Services, and when that is done, your reputation grows and is sustained and that is **SUCCESS**.

CONSISTENCY IS THE KEY:

C	WORD	IN THE HANDS OF THE ENVIRONMENT
O	TRUSTWORTHY	
N	RELIABLE	
S	DEPENDABLE	
I	USEFUL	
S	WANTED	
T	DEMAND	
E	POSITION	IN THE HANDS OF SELF
N	NEGOTIATE	
C	PROFIT	
Y	SUCCESS	

Ask this question to yourself? Are you in demand in your organisation, family, and community? If you are in demand, you can negotiate with them, otherwise not. Nobody deserves anything in life. You have to negotiate for it. There is a difference between Commitment and Interest. Yes I am interested in doing MBA. You will do it only when you get time. But when you are committed to do a MBA, you will find time and do it. When you are committed, you accept no excuses – only results.

In life you don't get what you deserve,
you get only what you negotiate

Begin practicing to honour your word. Start honouring all your agreements. Make small commitments and keep them. Character gets you out of bed, but only commitment moves you into action. A winner makes commitments, whereas a loser makes promises. **"Make commitments and stay committed".** A commitment is directly linked to your reputation.

What is the opposite of Commitment? It is Forced or Compelled. If you are forced to do a job your heart and head will not be there, but if you are committed to do it, all 3 H's Hand, Head and Heart will be present. When it comes to commitment, there are really four types of people:

Cop–outs: People who have no goals and do not commit.

Hold-outs: People who do not know if they can reach their goals, so they are afraid to commit.

Drop-outs: People who start towards a goal but quit when the going gets tough.

All-outs: Leaders who Set Goals, Commit to them, and Pay the Price to reach them.

> ***"Motivation is what gets you started. Commitment is what keeps you going." Jim Rohn***

When you break a commitment, it is understood as:

- The issue is not important to you
- Others are not important to you
- You yourself do not feel important to other issue.

'BUSY' is an excuse for not getting into a Commitment.

3. MOTIVATION:

The third meaning of 'Heart' means motivation. What is Motivation? Can I motivate you? Some may yes and some may say no. Others may be able to motivate you to a certain level. Look at the word "**Motivation**"; it is "**MOTIVE** for **ACTION**". What I or others can do for you is "**INSPIRE**" you; Inspiration is the changing of one's Thinking; whereas Motivation is Taking Action. YOU have to take Action. There is a reason or a motive for everything you do or don't do, for which you need to take some action. Other people or the management of a company can only give you an environment where you can start thinking, negatively or positively. They can give you a good salary, perks, promotion, appreciation, warnings, incentives etc., so that you can start thinking, yes I must do something.

You can take a horse to the water, but you can't make it drink. Therefore, others can inspire you temporarily, only you can motivate yourself; meaning that **motivation comes from within** – self motivation. Motivation can be negative and positive. Incentives, salary, increment, pat on back etc. are positive motivations, whereas fear is a negative motivation.

Can fear be a motivator? Of course, but not for a long time, may be for a shorter period. As long as there is work, there will be some motivation. The moment work finishes, they will be demotivated. As long as the motivator is present, work will go on; the moment the motivator disappears, so does the motivation. That is why we say that, motivation comes from within.

WHY DO YOU NEED MOTIVATION?

Because you want to achieve something; you will have many desires in life. So when you have a desire to become a corporate head, a great husband, great wife, have a bungalow, buy a car, you need to get yourselves motivated. It's like a fire, a burning desire in your belly, which is required. You have to add fuel every day; otherwise the fire will be doused. If there is no purpose or no desire in your life, no motivation is required. Bigger the desire, bigger the motivation. More fire, more heat; less fire, less heat. It's That Simple!

The employees should have qualities such as Responsibility, Commitment and Motivation. One has to be committed, because they are responsible for the organisation, their family, therefore they must be self-motivated. An incredible amount is spent towards training to inculcate these three qualities. But still the heart doesn't come into play. Put your Heart into the job and the job into your Heart. How can you bring your heart into the business?

Even in Ancient times, the concept of getting your heart in the business existed. The Princes were sent to Gurukul to receive education. They could even invite the Gurus to their Palace to impart education to the Rajkumars. But to take leadership of the kingdom, many things needed to be learned. In Gurukula, even the smallest jobs were to be done by the princes. In the ancient era, it was a value-based leadership. Today, that's missing. Spirituality brings a value based system. There is always some negativity in one's mind. How do you control it? In a Forest, the weeds (negativity) always grow without any effort. But to cultivate a garden (positivity), lot of efforts need to be made. Negative thoughts are born automatically. Positive thoughts take time and occur very rarely. That is the human nature.

Now circumstances are in control of you. You have to control your circumstances. The situation is changing. Times are changing. You have to do something to keep up with the pace. When you get good news you are in a good mood and when you get bad news, immediately your mind becomes restless and your mood becomes sour. It means the situation is controlling you. You need to have the presence of mind to not let that happen.

Competition is increasing. The problems keep on rising. You have to overcome them. Otherwise, they will overwhelm you. It is increasingly difficult to survive in the era of LPG, liberalization, privatization, and globalization. You have to take charge of your life. Even children feel incredibly stressed nowadays during their exams. That is why we witness an increase in suicide rates during that time. Difficult times are ahead. You have to take care of your stress; anger etc. otherwise you will collapse.

4. LISTENING:

The next ground rule is listening. There is a vast difference between hearing and listening. **Hearing is physical and listening is psychological.** Hearing implies, to take in the sounds with your ear. Listening makes you smarter after. The best way to convince other people is to listen to them and pay attention to what they say. It is a fact that when you give enough attention to what others say, they think that you are a very smart and intelligent person.

Listening is not just about hearing what the other person has to say. Listening involves patience, openness and the willingness to understand. It is more than just keeping your ear open. Often people pretend to listen to someone; in fact, usually they aren't listening at all. They are just waiting for the other person to pause for a fraction of second, so that they can dominate the conversation themselves. When you listen with your Ears, Eyes and Heart, it is known as dynamic listening. Talking is just sharing, while listening is caring. When you listen to your children you take care of them. When you listen to your spouse, your parents, you take care of them. For taking care of someone, you need to apply heart, eyes and ears. Switch off the TV when your loved ones talk to you, switch off the mobile when your boss or someone important is talking to you. This way they feel that you are taking care of them. Learn to listen. Opportunity sometimes knocks very softly.

Great people practice listening,
whereas ordinary people practice talking

Why don't people listen? It's because there is an excess in the supply of advice, without any demand for it. Some people have got a habit of selective listening.

STORY:

I would like to give you an example of selective listening. A medical doctor was invited as a guest speaker to address a group of alcoholics. He wanted to make a demonstration that would be powerful enough to make people realize that alcohol was injurious to their health. He had two containers, one with pure water and one with pure alcohol. He put an earthworm into the water and it swam beautifully and came up to the top. He put another earthworm into the alcohol and it died in front of everyone's eyes. He wanted to prove that this was what alcohol did to the insides of our body. He asked the group what the moral of the story was and one person from behind spoke up, "If you drink alcohol, you won't have any worms in your stomach." Was that the message? Of course, not. That was selective listening, i.e. we hear what we want to hear and not what is being said.

To relate effectively with your spouse, children, friends or colleagues, you must learn to listen. An open ear is the only believable sign of an open heart. Listening and participation is interrelated. When you participate, you listen and when you listen you participate. When you talk, you only say something that you already know. When you listen, you learn what others know and what you might not know. Successful people not only encourage others to talk but also keep their own mouths shut. If you can get others to talk enough, you can win their hearts.

Percentage of time we spend on each type of communication

Mode of Communication	**Formal years of Training**	**Percentage of Time used**
Writing	12 years	9%
Reading	6 – 8 years	16%
Speaking	1 – 2 years	30%
Listening	**0 – very few hours**	**45%**

Listening is the most powerful form of acknowledgment, a way of saying to the other person, "You are important."

Listening to everybody and listening to nobody are both erroneous

HOW DO YOU FEEL WHEN YOU WANTED SOMEBODY TO LISTEN TO YOU?

- They did more talking than listening.
- They disagreed with the first thing you said.
- They interrupted you at every step.
- They were impatient and completed every sentence you started.
- They were physically present but mentally absent.
- They heard you but didn't listen to you.
- They came to conclusions unrelated to the facts.
- They asked questions on unrelated topics.

LEVELS OF LISTENING:

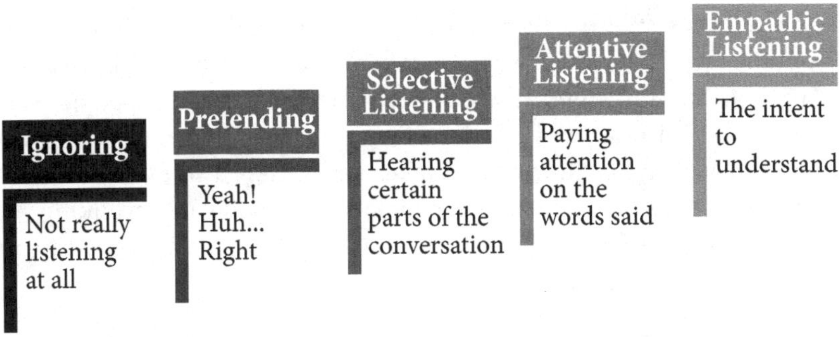

TIPS TO IMPROVE YOUR LISTENING SKILLS:

1. STOP TALKING – You cannot listen if you are talking.
2. REMOVE DISTRACTIONS – Don't doodle, tap or shuffle papers.
3. EMPATHISE WITH SPEAKER – Try to put yourself in their shoes so that you can see their point of view.
4. PUT THE SPEAKER AT EASE – Help them feel that they are free to talk. This is often called a permissive environment.
5. SHOW THEM THAT YOU WANT TO LISTEN – Do not read your mail while they talks. Listen to understand rather to oppose or reply.
6. LOOK AT THEIR EYES – Eye is the light house, a powerful media of communication.
7. HOLD YOUR TEMPER – An angry man gets the wrong meanings from words.
8. BE PATIENT – Allow plenty of time. Do not interrupt them. Don't start for the door or walk away.
9. SMILE – It will encourage the speaker
10. GO EASY ON ARGUMENT AND CRITICISM – This puts him on defensive. They may clam up or get angry. Do not argue – In argument nobody wins.
11. ASK RELEVANT QUESTIONS – This encourages them and shows you are listening.

5. ENTHUSIASM:

The other rule is - be Enthusiastic. The word "enthusiasm" comes from the Greek words "en theos" which means "God within". Enthusiasm is one of the most important characteristics of successful people. Have you observed how an enthusiastic sales girl in a departmental store greets you? Did you notice how a child takes keen interest in extra-curricular activities? If you are enthusiastic, people around you will start liking you. So never lose your enthusiasm. Enthusiasm and optimism can work miracles in life. Everyday affirm your enthusiasm.

Nothing great has ever been accomplished without enthusiasm.

How does one develop enthusiasm? Wake up in the morning like a spring. Think enthusiastically. Say to yourself "**Today is a great day and I am at my best**". Keep in mind that enthusiasm is contagious. Others will catch the enthusiasm you generate and soon the whole atmosphere will be a pleasant one. How do others know you are enthusiastic? It shows through the way you do and say everything. From your facial expression, gestures, posture, dress, style of walking, smile, way of talking, manners of greeting, clapping, hand shake etc. To become enthusiastic, act enthusiastic.

How do you develop Enthusiasm? Act and feel as if you are an enthusiastic person. Develop a good opinion of yourself and others. Practice eliminating dull, dead, unhealthy thoughts so that your mind is fresh and capable of developing enthusiasm. Affirm your enthusiasm every day. Always think, talk and live enthusiastically and then you will develop some.

No quality attracts people more than enthusiasm. Enthusiastic people radiate joy in what they do and make others want to participate too. Achievers must give the impression of being enthusiastic about everything they undertake.

Enthusiasm is a habit you must cultivate, to succeed in life. Most successful leaders developed this habit to become successful. They often point to enthusiasm as a key to their ability to lead and inspire their teams. Developing enthusiasm will take time, perseverance and a plan. Before you can be enthusiastic about something, you must first sell yourself on its merits and desirability. Accept the fact that nothing is ever absolutely perfect or imperfect.

A magnetized piece of iron can lift twelve times of its own weight; however, if it is demagnetized, it can't lift even a feather. Likewise, there are two kinds of people in the world – one is magnetized – they are so enthusiastic, full of confidence and faith, they are passionate, more courageous. On the other side, you will find people who are demagnetized – they are full of doubts and fears, no enthusiasm, no passion, no courage to do anything new. Whenever any opportunity comes, they withdraw themselves with lots of reasons, like people may laugh on them, what if they fail etc. See, opportunity has a bad habit of knocking the back door and if we don't capture it, it will exit from the front the door to the neighbour. Same opportunity will not come again. Opportunity only knocks the door, it doesn't break the door.

KEEP OURSELF ENTHUSED:

It is natural that almost all of us feel enthusiastic at the start of a new project. However, keeping the enthusiasm going over time is another issue, and is a problem for many people. Here are some ways to prevent our enthusiasm from flagging:

1. Use visual reminders of your purpose:

Visualization is simply a mental rehearsal. You create images in your mind of having or doing whatever it is that you want. You then repeat these images over and over again, Develop visual reminders of your goal and display it in such a way that every day you can see it.

2. Develop and start small steps:

It is easy to become discouraged if each step is big and requires lot of work. If you break the work into small steps, you can make some progress and measure it. Make a habit of breaking big projects into small steps. **A journey of a thousand miles start with a single step.**

3. Check off small steps:

As you take those tiny steps, check them off as you achieve each one and give yourself a pat on the back for your progress. Focus always on progress you have made as being just as important as the distance you have to go.

3. Avoid or Delete distractions:

Identify the time wasters and distracters while doing the project. Avoid them as much as possible. That list may include TV, computer games, gossiping, telephone, unwanted friends, social media etc. People say make a TO-DO LIST. I simply ask you to **Make a NOT TO DO LIST**, so that you will get an idea, where you are wasting your time.

4. Get enough rest:

Often we feel the need to work harder on a particular task, this results into more hours of work and less rest. However, the more number of hours you put in your work, the chances of getting fatigue and stress increase. Therefore, a good amount of rest or sleep is required.

5. Always Be happy and Think positively:

Happy people find good in the world. Positing thinkers are like fruits of all seasons. They are welcome everywhere.

STORY:

> Three boys were laying bricks. A passer-by asked the first boy, what are you doing? He replied, can't you see I am laying bricks? Then he asked the second boy the same question. The boy answered, "I am just making a living for which I get Rs. 50/- a day". And then the man asked the third boy, what are you doing? The third one said, "See I am building a beautiful temple"! Who do you think is more enthusiastic? Who is really enjoying the work? Whose productivity will be more? Of course the third one, because his work is directed towards an aim. It was observed that the productivity of the first person is 30%, the second 60% and the third is 90%. Now if there is a vacancy for a Supervisor coming up, who will be promoted? Naturally the third one, because he has got a vision, a goal and he knows the end use of the product. Success is something that comes to those who have always been enthusiastic.

6. SENSE OF OWNERSHIP:

The term ownership comes from a concept called psychological ownership, which means we can feel like we "own" something even if it is not a physical object. At work, you take ownership when you assume responsibility over a target or result. It is the opposite of passing the buck or making excuses.

Someone with a strong sense of ownership would say, "I need to do this task, I can do it, and I, therefore, have the responsibility of achieving success." Unfortunately, on average, a quarter of employees avoid this responsibility. In other words, they are not taking ownership of their work.

Five steps to help your employees take ownership in their work area:

1. Help your team feel like they belong:

When employees feel like they fit in, they are more likely to personally identify with their work. **"When you build a culture where people can be their authentic selves, they are going to bring their best work, their best ideas and their best people to your company."** Taking the time to understand each person's needs not only helps with productivity, but over time also builds the sense that this is the right team for them.

2. Let your team feel that they are owners:

Organisations with employee ownership "tend on average to match or exceed the performance of other similar firms." Even if you, as a manager, have zero control over your company's ownership program, there's still something important you can do for your team: make sure they understand it. It is definitely worth your time to make sure each person on your team understands the value of the program on a regular basis.

3. Align work, goals and purpose:

It is essential for employees to understand how their goals connect to the larger objectives of the organization. Employees in particular derive purpose and feel more engaged when they understand how their work directly contributes to the organization's success. Otherwise, they will have no motivation to stick around at all – let alone take ownership.

A strong sense of ownership and engagement is more likely to occur when the work being done is aligned with objectives. It needs to be crystal clear how these objectives impact the company's success. This has to do with the goals and objectives you set, but also to job title and job description.

4. Leave them, Don't micromanage:

Micromanaging erodes a sense of ownership. Instead of developing a sense of independence and feeling like they "own" figuring out how to achieve what's needed, employees learn to rely on you as a manager. Worse, it undermines their confidence that they can do the task, or at the very least that they can do it to their manager's liking.

Holding employees accountable is a powerful way to build a sense of ownership, so set clear expectations about the results you want. Provide them with any help or guidance they ask for, but don't be afraid to let them fail. Resist the urge to go in and fix things yourself – or tell your employees how they should work.

It's hard to take ownership of someone else's recipe/playbook. If they own the result, they need to own creating the playbook, and they also need to own asking for help if they feel stuck. Make that clear.

5. Get your team's input on the things that impact their work:

If you want someone to own something, you need to empower them to have that responsibility. That means giving them a say on the strategy, projects and processes that impact their work. You can't tell someone they own the result and then make a decision without them that affects their ability to hit said result.

Giving your team a voice also helps build a sense of ownership. Having the ability to influence strategy, project or job design helps employees feel more connected to their own work and the results that they are accountable for.

If you are not fired with Enthusiasm,
you will be fired with Enthusiasm.

DREAM PRECEDES SUCCESS

WHAT IS SUCCESS?

During my interaction in training programmes, I often ask the participants, do you want to be successful in life? Without any ambiguity, everyone agrees that they want to be successful in all walks of life. Then I ask them, are you becoming successful the way you want to? Here I get mixed response from my participants – some say 'yes', some say 'no' and some agree that they are successful in some areas of life they aren't in some. Everybody wants success in life. And no doubt you all are getting some success, but not exactly the way you want to. In some spheres of life, surely you will have success, but not in others. May be you are a success in your professional life, but you can't seem to achieve the same amount of success in your family or social life. Many be successful in social and spiritual life, may not be successful in financial life.

Ultimately you want to be successful in all areas that is what you are working for day and night. Why aren't you attaining success in all areas? There are basically three rules of life, which you should follow to achieve success. Each rule is built up on one another and therefore, it has to be followed and practiced that way.

RULE NO.1 - YOUR FUTURE SHOULD BE GREATER THAN YOUR PAST:

Do you agree? Yes, but often it doesn't happen like that. Your future may be growing brighter, but not with the intensity you want. It's a snail's progress. So what do you need to do to make it better? So many preach that we should work hard, that our goals are not clear, that we aren't putting efforts, lethargic, not disciplined, etc. All these are factors which hinder your progress. But apart from all these hindrances, the most important one is that, **YOU ARE LIVING IN THE PAST**. Most of your time is spent in thinking about the past. The past has ended, and you no more live there. Those who live the in past don't enjoy the present and aren't getting to their future. Past is like a cancelled cheque, present is the currency and future is a promissory note. Today is a gift to you that is why it is called present day.

I can't go back to yesterday
– because I was a different person then.

You keep on thinking about the past – my previous organisation was good; my ex-boss was a nice gentleman; in a lighter way – my first wife is far better than the current one; the previous policies were better, the previous neighbour was perfect and the past government was efficient. Past is a raw material and you should learn from those bad experiences and failures. There is no point in spending time there. See you have already spent twenty four hours yesterday, so do you want to give any extra hour from today to the past. You are absent in the present and present in the past and that is why you are not getting to your future.

What got you here won't get your there.

Whatever knowledge, skill, abilities and talents you have accumulated till now is fantastic. To do the current job, these qualities may be good enough. But your current knowledge, skill, abilities and talents cannot take you to the future. Change is inevitable, the technology, the policies, environment, politics, hierarchy, strategy, etc. changes every time. But what if you don't change? If you have still the same knowledge and skill, it will become obsolete.

Your behaviour and attitude is absolutely perfect today. However, this will not take you to future. The behaviour you had with your child when he or she was 5 years old or a teenager will not work now. You might have been harsh with the child and that may have been ok at that time, but now the child has become a teenager or an adult, so you can't still behave the same way. They have changed a lot, but you have not. Therefore, the children are not happy with you, with the way you behave now. Your spouse is unhappy with you, because even after spending so many years of marriage together, you have not changed your attitude or your behaviour. They may be expecting something entirely different from you.

Therefore, if you want to make your future better in any area of your life, whether it's personal, family, social, spiritual, financial, physical; **from today onwards do something new, something great, something big, something extra and something more.** Otherwise your future will not change. Live each day in the present and make it beautiful.

And that is also a form of creativity; you are always creating something new.

I spent 24 hours yesterday and I don't want to spend few more hours from today in the past.

DO I GROW EVERYDAY?

DO I ENRICH MYSELF EVERYDAY?

OR

DO I DIMINISH EVERYDAY?

DO I GET 'RUST-OUT' EVERYDAY?

RULE NO.2 – YOUR CONTRIBUTION SHOULD BE GREATER THAN YOUR REWARD:

From the first rule, you have seen that everybody wants success. Now how can you make your future better if you don't contribute towards it? Are you contributing your 100% in your organisation? Are you contributing your 100% towards your family, in your personal and social life? No. Many people don't contribute their 100% in any area of their life.

But I believe that you are contributing 100% in all spheres of life. You are supposed to contribute 100%. But that is not enough. If everybody contributes their all, who will rise up in the organisation? So if you want to grow in life, you have to contribute more than 100%. Whatever you are contributing is not enough to make your future better.

Your customers want something new, something better and something extra, and if you don't give more than 100% to your customers, they will go to your competitors. Your competitor is always eyeing you, the moment your contribution is same as before or less, your competitors will gain, because they are always providing that something new, better, and extra to the customers. Who is your customer? Your family, boss, subordinates, peers, friends, community members are all your internal customers. If you spend a half an hour of quality time extra with your child, wife, or parents, you are contributing more to their life and your future in that area will definitely be successful. The same way, if you spend half an hour extra in mentoring your subordinates, giving additional output to the organisation, your future will be bright.

Therefore, **from today onwards contribute something more, better, extra and new in your customer's life, in your organisation, in your family, in your community and in your own personal life.** The moment you contribute more, your future will be great. The moment you contribute something extra, you future will be extraordinary.

When you cease to make a contribution, you begin to die.

RULE NO.3 – YOUR LEARNING SHOULD BE GREATER THAN YOUR EXPERIENCE:

You have now seen that, to make your future successful, you need to contribute. No doubt, you are contributing, but what you contribute is what you already know; and if you want to contribute something more, something new, you need to learn something more and something new, it's as simple as that. With the same knowledge and skill, you will not be able to contribute more than before. Therefore, **from today onwards, learn something new, big, better, and more, so that your contributions are more, new and better.**

When you learn, what do you receive? You receive knowledge. In fact when you read a book, or attend a training session, you get some data or information and not knowledge. You tend to forget most of the information pretty soon. You have to read and revise this information till it becomes your knowledge. You have lots of knowledge on varied subjects like politics, sports, films, professional work, religions etc. That is the knowledge you have with you, because you know it. This knowledge will not prompt you to learn further or will not take you to a better future. You should have one more type of knowledge, what is that?

An investment in knowledge pays the best interest.
– Benjamin Franklin

The most important knowledge that you should have is **the knowledge about that which you don't know**. So there are two types of knowledge – **one is what you know and the other is what you don't know**. Once you realise what you don't know, what will you do? You will learn it. Without recognizing what you don't know, what are you going to learn – nothing. So it is very important for you to understand which is that knowledge that you don't know and should acquire?

And the question is how do you realise what you don't know? It is only possible when you ask yourself, where do you want to go in your life and what you want to acquire along the way? If you want to go to Singapore, you will find out the details through various sources. Make your goal crystal clear. Let's say you want to get promoted to the next available position. Now you should understand what qualifications, knowledge, skills, abilities, talents, exposure and experience is required to obtain that position? Once you get these details, you can learn and prepare accordingly to go up on the ladder of success.

Is knowledge powerful? Many people say that knowledge is powerful. I say no, it's not so. If 5 kilograms of gold and a 10 rupees coin is lying deep down under the ocean, what is its value, it is zero. When will its value be determined? Only when you take it out and use it. Therefore knowledge is not powerful; use of knowledge is what gives you power. Knowledge is only a hidden power; it has potential only when you use it. Who uses the knowledge for their gain is what matters? Take a knife for instance, who uses it, and for what is what determines its value. A doctor uses a knife to heal somebody and a criminal uses it to kill somebody. Similarly knowledge does not hold the power to take action. **The great end of life is not knowledge, but action.**

Knowledge with action converts adversity into prosperity.
- A.P.J. Abdul Kalam

Nobody will grow in their life, just because they have acquired knowledge. When you use or apply your knowledge repeatedly, it becomes a skill. So whatever knowledge you acquire in life, apply it, practice it, then it will become a skill.

Practice doesn't make the man perfect, but improved.

Once you have the necessary knowledge and skill, your attitude will change. What is attitude? It is the feeling that you have towards some person or object. When you meet someone or see something, you have certain feelings towards that. What are the likely feelings we have - happiness, sad, sorrow, courage, angry, confidence, amazement, etc. Attitude is contagious. It's like the flu. Any time you want to 'catch something' just go where it is prevalent.

How would you feel today if your knowledge and skill were better than yesterday?

You would feel great, you would feel confident and you would feel courageous. Therefore, if you want to have a better attitude, you have to learn every day, something new, something great and something extra. **If you want to feel good, you have to feed good! SO FEED GOOD - FEEL GOOD.** Without feeding something good every day, you won't feel good.

Learning ↗ **(FEEDING)** – leads to

⇓ ⇒ Collection of Data or Information, and when you read and revise it, it leads to

Knowledge – Two types – Knowing and Not knowing

⇓ ⇒ When you practice the knowledge, it leads to

Skill - And when you have knowledge and skill better than yesterday, it will lead to

⇓

Attitude ⟶ **(FEELING)**

If you feel good or your attitude is good, you can always learn, you can contribute and your future will be greater than your past.

Never stop learning;
for when we stop learning, we stop growing.

ARE YOU SUCCESSFUL?

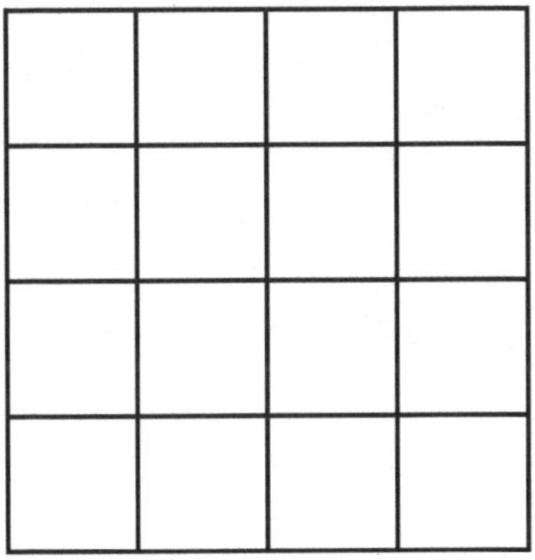

How many squares can you see? Initially you may say 16 or 17, but look at it from all angles, small and big squares; gradually you will find 20, 24, 28 and 30. In fact, it has 30 squares. At first look, you may have seen only 16, 17 or even 20; this is what happens with your life. You can't see your potential, your capabilities and what future you have, unless somebody tells you about it. If you look within yourself and introspect within, you will find lots of capabilities and huge potential inside you. But somehow you do not look within yourself and wonder why you aren't attaining success?

I often ask in my training sessions, what do you ultimately want in your life? Most of the participants say, life should be pretty good, wonderful health, prosperity, good friends, social status, sound financial security, good family relationships, success, happiness, peace of mind, and many other good things in life. But when I ask them, does wealth bring you happiness or peace of mind; does success bring you happiness or health, they often say, not necessarily. Finally everybody agrees that success and happiness should go along together in life. And they also agree that success is a relative term. The meaning of success may differ from person to person. For some, success may mean many wonderful and positive things, for somebody else success may mean money, for others it may mean good health, a beautiful home, giving children and all the advantages, a peaceful life, winning admiration, free from frustration, fear, failure etc.

To be Happy
Healthy
Secure &
To have friends
Peace of Mind
Good
Hope

For me success means striving to improve myself continuously by emotionally, physically, financially, socially, psychologically, academically, professionally, family-wise. If my child becomes better than me, then I am a successful father.

So let us define success this way - **"Success is the Progressive Realization of a Worthy Goal without violating the Rights of others".** It is the direction in which you are travelling; it is an achievement of worthy and value based goals without violating the rights of others; and in the process of achieving, adding value in others life". Success implies Striving to improve yourself continuously in all respects emotionally, Physically, Financially, Socially, Psychologically, Family-wise.

Definition of success differs from person to person. No one has ever defined success, such that it is applicable to everyone. You can get what you want instead of having to want what you have. Success can be had once you develop belief in yourself. But first, you must believe. Success is easy once you believe.

Success and Happiness are not a matter of chance but of choice

You already possess the wonderful qualities required for success. Make a list of qualities that you have; you will find you have a well-polished character, faith, integrity, honesty, love and loyalty. The only missing link may be that you may not have a goal to meet and the right kind of mental attitude to achieve that goal. All you have to do is to use the qualities you have and give each quality a chance to grow, because the basic principle of life says, **'the more you use of what you have, the more you will have to use'.**

Success is a journey from survival to significance. Everybody on earth wants success. Nobody wants a life crawling, spent in mediocrity.

Your Highway to Success

Your Highway to success is not straight;
There are Curves called Failures;
Loops called Confusions;
Speed bumps called Friends;
Red lights called Enemies;
Caution lights called Family;
But….if you have a Spare wheel called Determination;
And Engine called Perseverance;
And Insurance policy called Faith;
And a Driver called God;
You will make it to a Place called Success.

Success comes in CANs, not in CANNOTs

You cannot achieve success unless you begin. The first step is to begin. We must begin if an opportunity of growth arises. On a ten level scale, if I am at level two in any field and desire to move to five or more, I must first take the step towards level three and so on. There is a saying **"A long journey starts with a single step".**

START is the ART of SUCCESS

Once a greedy man asked God for a boon - God, please grant me a winning lottery. God said that within a year, you would win a big lottery. He was so happy. He was just counting the days and that one-year passed by quickly. With a dejected heart, he again went and appealed to God. God, one year has passed by and I still did not win any lottery. Then the God said, man, you should have at least bought a lottery ticket.

This is what happens to us. The problem with most of us is that we have unrealistic demands and expectation and want immediate results without even beginning to work on achieving the goal.

FULL FORM OF SUCCESS:

S = SINCERITY
U = URGE
C = COURAGE
C = CONFIDENCE
E = EARNESTNESS
S = SERIOUSNESS
S = SOBERNESS

FORMULA OF SUCCESS:

WxIxSxH →

Will Power
Initiative
Set Purpose
Hard Work

Success is a journey from **WISH** to **FULFILMENT.** To get from wish to fulfilment, you have to go a long way. Simply wishing for something is passive and inactive. It does not have any influence and cannot produce results. Wishing is different from dreaming. Wishing is just an ideal pastime with no efforts behind it. But dreaming is followed by an action plan to produce results. Hard work by itself will not lead you to success, unless you have a purpose to achieve and for which you must have information, knowledge and the will power to do what is necessary. Everyone likes to win but how many are willing to put in the effort and time prepares to win? It takes sacrifice and self-discipline.

The road to success is always under construction. Either you are constructing your road to success or cleaning the site to begin construction or perhaps you are searching for the right site to construct the road.

You know success is most enjoyable when it has been won against all odds.

IS IT POSSIBLE TO MEASURE YOUR SUCCESS?

People normally say yes, you can measure your success rate by comparing it with others. To a certain extent, as a parameter, you can say that you are progressing, when compared to others. Suppose a student secured the highest marks and the first rank in a class of 35 students. Is she successful? Many people will say, yes, she is a success as far as education and marks are concerned, in her class.

Now if I say that the child got only 19/100 marks, then people will say - no he is not successful. Even though he may have received the highest marks in the class, he is not successful. Number one doesn't mean success. Compared to other students he is successful. But that is not success. Success is measured not by how you are doing compared with others, but compared with what you are capable of doing.

Don't compare yourself with anyone in the world. If you compare, you are insulting yourself.

Your capability, ability, potential and target are the criteria for comparing your success. It is competing against yourself. It is making your own records better and better. For example, there is a teacher having B.Ed qualification getting Rs. 25,000 in a school, whereas another teacher with the same qualification, passed from the same university, belonging from the same village with same experience is getting Rs.40,000 salary. There is a doctor who charges Rs.50 as consulting fees and another one charges Rs.500. There is a trainer who charges Rs.500 per day as professional fee, the other one charges 50,000. Now where is the difference? Is it because the teacher who gets lower salary doesn't have the qualification, experience, and capability? Is it because the doctor who charges Rs.50 doesn't have the capability or experience? Does the trainer who charges less, not have the skill to deliver. No, they each have all the requirements that the school, hospital or institute needs. But the other teacher, doctor or trainer has realized their potential, and increased their **DESIRE** to grow more and use the potential they have. They have amplified their desire along with their knowledge and skill. Simple desire would be insufficient to grow; you have to increase your knowledge and skill along with a burning desire to come up in the life.

DESIRE IS THE STARTING POINT OF ALL SUCCESS – THE BURNING DESIRE. JUST LIKE A SMALL FIRE CANNOT GIVE MUCH HEAT, A WEAK DESIRE CANNOT PRODUCE GREAT RESULTS.

To earn more, you have to learn more.

You are born for doing better than this. You are meant to live at a higher standard than you are living right now. Don't be satisfied with what you have and settle for less. God doesn't want you to be good enough. He wants you to use your full potential. Keep stretching forward towards the next level. Definite aim- definite goal-definite destination, this is the first condition of success.

STORY:

Once upon a time there was a bird which could talk in five languages. One person thought of having it and searched throughout the world. Finally he found it in a pet store. Since he had to go for a tour, he asked the store owner, whether he could deliver the bird to his house. On paying the amount and giving the address, he left for a tour. After coming back from the tour, he asked his wife, whether any person has delivered a bird. She said, yes. The husband asked her where it was. She replied, it is in the oven. He was angry and shouted at her, are you a lunatic? You know that bird could speak five languages and it is the only one of its kind in the world, and you put it in the oven. That lady shouted back, how would I know that the bird could speak five languages; till this second the bird did not utter a single word.

See friends, you are all like that bird, you have the capability, ability and the potential to do many things, but you don't speak up. How will the world know unless you speak up? You need to speak, you need to publicize yourself, let the world know you exist and you are there to take up any challenges. When you challenge, you become unchallenged.

Opportunities do not come to you; you need to go to the opportunities.

The universe is like a river. The river keeps on flowing. It doesn't bother whether you are happy or sad, successful or a failure, good or bad, it just keeps flowing. Some people go down the river and cry, some are happy. But the river doesn't care. It just keeps flowing. You can use it and enjoy it or you can jump in and drown. The universe that you live in can support you or destroy you; it is your interpretation and positive or negative thinking that affects the results. You can only receive what your mind is capable of accepting.

You can go to the river of success with a teaspoon, with a cup, with a bucket, with a barrel, or with a tanker. You can also construct a pipeline. It doesn't make the universe poor. You went to river with a small bucket to fetch water. Then, you cry when others fill the water in their barrels or tankers. The river did not deny you. It is you who decided to go with a small bucket. To go with a barrel or a tanker, you have to work harder, for which you are not ready.

BETTER YOUR OWN RECORD:

Success is about competing against ourselves, making our records better and better. **What is winning?** People usually say, winning is about reaching first or defeating others, etc. Suppose you are running a 100 meter race today, you complete it in one minute and you reach first and become the winner. Next day in another 100 meter race, you reached first again, but this time you took 1 minute and 15 seconds. Is it a win or a loss for you. For others you may be a winner, but for you it's a defeat. Another day you run another 100 metre race, but this time you finish it in 45 seconds but failed to be in first position. Somebody else finished the race first. Is it a loss or a win for you? Of course, it is a win for you; others may think that you lost. So winning is not reaching first or defeating others, it is improving yourselves every day, making yourselves better and better every day in integrity, intelligence and energy. You go on improving your performance day by day in all areas. Even if it's a small improvement in your communication, in your attitude, in your personality, you should go on improving in hundreds of such areas. Winning is just a by-product.

Please make the habit of jumping into the river of success with positive thoughts. The universe has lot to offer. No one can impede you from the journey towards success. You will come out the winner. Always make the habit of constructing a pipeline. The truth is that you can have anything you want if you start thinking and believing that you can have it.

Thomas Alva Edison said, if we did all the things we are capable of doing, we would literally astound ourselves. Anyone who sets out to be less than he is capable of will be unhappy for the rest of their life. We all have dreams when we join a job or start a business that I want to become a CEO, I want to have a big bungalow, 100 crores rupees net profit etc. But what happens after that is most people forget their dreams and get involved in various distractions. And when they look back, after putting in 10 or 15 years of hard work, the find their growth was slow and that they have achieved much less than they set out to, though the potential to become more is still in them.

STORY:

Once a businessman from Bangalore phoned his counterpart at Mumbai and said, can you please come to Bangalore by tomorrow evening, a big contract has to be finalized and signed. Next day this person went to Mumbai airport and bought a ticket. Since there was an announcement that the flight to Bangalore is delayed, he was reading a newspaper. Suddenly he saw a weighing machine and he stood on it and inserted a two-rupee coin. A message came from the machine that you are Mr. Arun, your age is 45, your height is 5.9', your weight is 70 kgs and you are going to Bangalore by flight number 707. He was astonished, how this machine could get all the details. He wondered, maybe somebody was watching him. He punched the machine couple of times and again inserted a coin. The same message came. He was still puzzled, and wondered what to do. He called all the passengers and asked them to surround him so no computer or camera could watch him. He inserted another coin, again the same message.

This time in frustration he went to rest room and changed his cloth and dressed like a lady and inserted another coin. The same message, you are Mr. Arun, your age is 45, your height is 5.9', your weight is 70 kgs but the flight number 707 has already left for Bangalore.

He forgot what he came to the airport for. Similarly, somewhere we all waver into distractions and our all dreams then dissipate into nothing. We forget our dreams and goals in between.

People don't fail because they lack ability or intelligence, but because they lack the 8 'Ds':

DREAM
DESIRE
DIRECTION
DEDICATION
DISCIPLINE
DETERMINATION
DEVOTION
DEADLINE

Successful people do not have to be twice as smart as their peers. They have to be only a little more intelligent, have a little more drive and a little more ambition. For achieving success, you have to prepare very well. What were you created for? What is your destiny? What were you meant to do with your life? Success is not merely a question of luck or genius, it depends on hard work, sustained toil and intelligent application of efforts on your part. Above all it is rooted to your ability to persist despite odds, facing setbacks and possible adverse circumstances.

The Dictionary is the only place where SUCCESS comes before WORK.

If success means attainment of one's goals, does failure mean non-attainment of one's goals? If success means earning loads of money or getting recognition, does failure mean being penniless or faceless in a crowd? Certainly not.

DEFINITION OF FAILURE - Failure means, not trying to achieve one's goals or having no goals at all. Failure doesn't imply the shattering of all your dreams. Failure means not dreaming big. Failure implies to lead life without the willingness to live to the fullest. People who consider themselves as pawns, helpless beings are Raw Failures. Success is all about bouncing back when we fall down.

THE SINGLE MOST INGREDIENT IN THE RECIPE OF SUCCESS:

Those who never fail are those who never try

"It is impossible to live without failing at something, unless you live so cautiously that you might as well not have lived at all - in which case, you fail by default." - J. K. Rowling

If you are still wondering what ingredient is it that I am talking about here, then let me tell you – it is failure! Failure can be a challenge. It can take a toll on your sense of well-being. But, the truth is we all have failed at some point in our life. And, that's the ultimate truth. Some people fail in their career, some in their relationships, and so on!

Can anyone honestly say that they have never made any mistakes in life or never failed at something? I know I have had my fair share of failures. I have failed more than I would like to admit. But, what I have learned is that every failure is a jump-off point for growth and learning.

You need to look at failure with that mentality. If you don't, it will be a huge anchor weighing you down at one place and keeping you stuck in a rut. "Are you looking for ways to convert your project failures into a success? If yes, then you must try". It's ok to fail.

Failures suck! Nobody likes them. And, when you are faced with them, you start being too hard on yourself. You start thinking you are not competent enough. A way to deal with failure is to first accept the fact that it is absolutely ok and perfectly fine to fail sometimes at certain things. Just because you could not succeed at something, doesn't mean that you are incompetent. It only means that there is more to learn or that perhaps what you failed at was never truly your calling.

Failure is essential:

It is not just some philosophical cliché, but the truth of life. Thomas Edison's thousand failed attempts before finally creating the light bulb is the perfect example that proves just how true this statement is. He did think of those thousand unsuccessful attempts as failures. He just figured that this many avenues will not work.

Failure is often a disguised opportunity:

Failure is just a moment in time. It is not a continuous thing and definitely not permanent. It is always temporary just like everything else in life. Besides, when you are entangled thinking about where you went wrong and what you could have done to avoid failures, you fail to see the bigger picture that is slowly starting to form.

Failure may seem like a negative thing in that moment, but mostly it acts like a doorway to latent opportunities. Sometimes really big ones. But, you have to give things some time and wait it out before you're able to connect all the dots and realize why failure was necessary.

It gets you out of your comfort zone:

Sometimes all we need is a little push in the direction of success. Failure can give you that push. Often you don't feel motivated enough to get out of your comfort zone or try out things that might have the potential to change everything. Sometimes a step back can actually be a positive thing. It gives you that mental boost to see where you are going wrong and self-analyse where you are lacking and what can be done to improve yourself.

Even in the words of Bill Gates - "Success is a lousy teacher. It seduces smart people into thinking they can't lose."

Failure is the real teacher, because it tells you what does not work so you don't repeat those mistakes. You all want to keep succeeding without making any mistakes. But, that involves such cautious thinking and calculated planning at every step that you almost lead a life full of fear. And, while failure may not seem like anything positive, fearful thinking aimed at avoiding failures is not very positive either.

Failure helps you practice resilience:

Perhaps the most crucial trait one needs in life is resilience. But, you cannot develop it if everything is going your way - if somehow you always keep on succeeding; although that rarely happens, unless you happen to be very lucky. Failure teaches you to be flexible in your dealings and it makes you realize that things are highly uncertain. It makes you more realistic about what to expect. You learn that the desire for success brings certain expectations. You learn to manage them and don't feel disappointed even if you can't meet them.

F E A R – FORGET EVERYTHING AND RUN or FACE EVERYTHING AND RISE

SUCCESS is the time to redefine GOALS;
FAILURE is the time to redefine MEANS

All these personalities are failures, but bounced back:

- A man had very little formal education as a child, attending school only for a few months. He was taught reading, writing, and arithmetic by his mother because his schoolmaster called him slow. At thirteen he took a job as a newsboy, selling newspapers. Failed in everything which he did and became... **Thomas Alva Edison**, the inventor of the electric bulb. When Thomas Edison invented the light bulb, he tried over 2000 experiments before he got it to work. A young reporter asked him how it felt to fail so many times. He said, "I never failed once. I invented the light bulb. It just happened to be a 2000-step process."
- A school teacher scolded a boy for not paying attention to his mathematics and for not being able to solve simple problems. She told him that you would not become anybody in life. The boy was.... Ordinary Patent Clerk **Albert Einstein.**
- Failed in business at the age of 21; was defeated in a legislative race at age 22; failed again in business at age 24; overcame the death of his sweetheart at age 26; had a nervous breakdown at age 27; lost a congressional race at age 34; lost a senatorial race at age 45; failed in an effort to become vice-president at age 47; lost a senatorial race at age 49; and **Abraham Lincoln** was elected president of the United States at age 52.
- A small boy, the fifth amongst seven siblings of a poor father, was selling newspapers in a small village to earn his living. He was not exceptionally smart at school but was fascinated by religion and rockets. The first rocket he built crashed. A missile that he built crashed multiple times and he was made a butt of ridicule. He is the person to

have scripted the Space Odyssey of India single-handedly. He is **Dr. A P J Abdul Kalam**.

- Officials rejected a candidate for a news broadcasters post since his voice was not fit for a news broadcaster. He was also told that with his obnoxiously long name he would never be famous and he became **Amitabh Bachchan.**
- As a young cartoonist, **Walt Disney** faced many rejections from newspaper editors, who said he had no talent. One day a minister at a church hired him to draw some cartoons. Disney was working out of a small mouse infested shed near the church. After seeing a small mouse he was inspired. That was the start of Mickey Mouse. Walt Disney.
- In 1962, four nervous young musicians played their first record audition for the executives of the Decca Recording Company. The executives were not impressed. While turning down this group of musicians, one executive said, "We don't like their sound. Groups of guitars were on the way out to become **The Beatles.**
- In the 1940s, another young inventor named Chester Carlson took his idea to 20 corporations, including some of the biggest in the country. They all turned him down. In 1947, after 7 long years of rejections, he finally got a tiny company in Rochester, NY, the Haloid Company, to purchase the rights to his invention - an electrostatic paper-copying process. Haloid became.... **Xerox Corporation**.
- Born as Shivaji Rao Gaekwad, struggled with an impoverished life-style during his childhood, and then joining the then-Bangalore Transport Service as a bus conductor after doing many petty jobs, moved to Chennai to seek a career in acting and joined the Madras Film Institute with the help of a friend, and became none other than **Rajnikanth**.
- Sons of a father who served as a muezzin in a mosque in Baroda, these two brothers went against their father's desire to be Islamic scholars and started playing cricket on the grounds off and inside the mosque, later known as Pathan brothers **Yusuf and Irfan**.
- His Father died before his birth; his mother died in his very young age; no one in the world taught him; He faced and fought against

many trials. At the age of 12 he wrote in his room, I am the greatest and he became great. He is **Mohammed Ali**, three times world Boxing champion.

- Popularly known as 'muchhad Paanwala', **Jaishankar Tiwari**, is the man behind the amazing and mouth watering paan (betel leaf) in Mumbai. Most people zip by in their fancy cars, make a quick stop at Muchhad's to grab a few paans and zip off again. This millionaire paanwala, having his own website, is legendary for his intimidating moustache and ornate paans, all maintain big and long moustaches that almost touches their ears.
- His parents were quite poor. During his school days, he used to go across river Ganga, near Varanasi to attend his classes. He did not have enough money to pay for boat, hence, he used to swim across keeping the bag of books on his head. When he was Minister of Railways, a major train accident took place. He owned up the moral responsibility and resigned. Despite requests for reconsideration from Jawaharlal Nehru, he did not budge. When he was Minister without portfolio, Nehruji asked him to go to Kashmir, on the issue of holy relics. It was peak winter and he did not have enough woollen clothes. Pt Nehru gave his own overcoat to him. When he was Prime Minister, India faced shortage of food grains. He appealed to all the Indians to skip evening meals every Monday. Such was the magic of his appeal that all restaurants, bakeries etc used to remain closed on Monday evenings in most cities. When he was Prime Minister, he took loan to buy an Ambassador Car for his personal use. When he died, some part of the loan was still outstanding. He was **Lal Bahadur Shastri**.
- This is the story of a person who was born with no arms or legs. Growing up was not easy for him because he was often teased in school. His parents chose not to send him to a "special" school for children with disabilities. Rather he attended an integrated school as any other child, decision which was hard for him to accept but in the long run helped him face and overcome many obstacles. By 10 years of age he became so depressed about his condition that he contemplated suicide. He would pray for the miracle of limbs. When this didn't happen he began to be grateful for being alive.

One life-changing experience came when his mother showed him a newspaper cut-out of a man who used his disability to inspire others. It was then than he knew his life's purpose. So at 17 he began to address groups as a motivational speaker. He later went to college and graduated at 21 with a double major in Administration and Finances! His motto has become "**Never Give Up**". Life without limits is how he has chosen to live his life now. He's even writing a book entitled - **No Arms, No Legs, No worries!** Being limbless has not stopped him from becoming an international motivational speaker, preacher and director an organization he founded, He swims, surfs and lives his life to the fullest. He is **Nick Vujicic** from Australia.

- A little girl - the 20th of 22 children, was born prematurely and her survival was doubtful. When she was 4 years old, she contracted double pneumonia and scarlet fever, which left her with a paralyzed left leg. At age 9, she removed the metal leg brace she had been dependent on and began to walk without it. By 13 she had developed a rhythmic walk, which doctors said was a miracle. That same year she decided to become a runner. She entered a race and came in last. For the next few years every race she entered, she came in last. Everyone told her to quit, but she kept on running. One day she actually won a race; and then another. From then on she won every race she entered. Eventually this little girl **Wilma Rudolph**, went on to win three Olympic gold medals.

- **Sudha Chandran** was born to family in Chennai, South India. She completed her Masters in Economics from Mumbai. On one of her return trips from Mumbai to Chennai she met with an accident resulting in the amputation of her right leg. She was given an artificial leg and despite this terrible disability, she became one of the most accomplished and acclaimed dancers of the Indian Subcontinent. She has received and still receives invitations to perform all over the world. She has been honored with numerous awards and has performed all over the world. She appears often on Hindi television and in films.

- A guy who is so obsessed with his girlfriend that he came to Mumbai and searched for her with only the information that she loved swimming. He sold his Pentax camera for Rs 10,000, as he combed beaches with hope and prayer that he would locate her, sleeping on the park benches, and cleaning and bathing in the hotel bathrooms. His friends lost hope and purchased tickets with the balance remaining money while he for the last time combed the north Mumbai beaches and luckily found her. Sitting for long time at the Marine Drive in Mumbai, he promised that one day he would rule the city of Mumbai. This is none other than today's superstar **Shah Rukh Khan**. Needless to say picture abhi baki hai…mere dost.

- This is the story of a person who lost his television manufacturing venture called Apollo Television during 1984 Sikh riots. He was forced to work as an insurance surveyor to pay off his loans. But his spirit was not broken, he was determined to rise again and he started his jeans manufacturing business, called Charlie Creations, with his brother-in-law in 1991. He has learnt his lessons and decided to sell from his own exclusive stores so that he had control on his brands. He became **Mr. D.P. S. Kohli**, owner of Koutons, which has 1000 exclusive stores almost 4 times of any other apparel brand.
- When you look at **Arnold Schwarzenegger**, bristling with muscles and physical fitness, you do not say; 'WOW, he sure is lucky to be born with such a great physique. You know that Arnold, six times Mr. Olympia and five times Mr. Universe has worked out for more than 20 years, investing thousands of hours pumping iron to build his body to be point where he wins prizes and starring roles in high-grossing movies. He has the same 10 muscles on his body that you and I have. He has simply worked on them for longer and far more seriously than you and I could ever imagine. He has paid an incredible price to develop himself physically, and he is enjoying the rewards.

Karoly Takacs : A Hero, An Inspiration

You've probably never heard of him. However, in Hungary, he's a national hero – everybody there knows his name and his incredible story. After reading his story, you'll never forget him.

In 1938, Karoly Takacs of the Hungarian Army, was the top pistol shooter in the world. He was expected to win the gold in the 1940 Olympic Games scheduled for Tokyo. Those expectations vanished one terrible day just months before the Olympics. While training with his army squad, a hand grenade exploded in Takacs' right hand, and Takacs' shooting hand was blown off.

Takacs spent a month in the hospital depressed at both the loss of his hand, and the end to his Olympic dream. At that point most people would have quit. And they would have probably spent the rest of their life feeling sorry for themselves. Most people would have quit but not Takacs. Takacs was a winner. Winners know that they can't let circumstances keep them down. They understand that life is hard and that they can't let life beat them down. Winners know in their heart that quitting is not an option.

Takacs did the unthinkable; he picked himself up, dusted himself off, and decided to learn how to shoot with his left hand! His reasoning was simple. He simply asked himself, "Why not?"

Instead of focusing on what he didn't have – a world class right shooting hand, he decided to focus on what he did have – incredible mental toughness, and a healthy left hand that with time, could be developed to shoot like a champion.

For months Takacs practiced by himself. No one knew what he was doing. Maybe he didn't want to subject himself to people who most certainly would have discouraged him from his rekindled dream.

In the spring of 1939 he showed up at the Hungarian National Pistol Shooting Championship. Other shooters approached Takacs to give him their condolences and to congratulate him on having the strength to come watch them shoot. They were surprised when he said, "I didn't come to watch, I came to compete." They were even more surprised when Takacs won!

The 1940 and 1944 Olympics were cancelled because of World War II. It looked like Takacs' Olympic Dream would never have a chance to realize itself. But Takacs kept training and in 1944 he qualified for the London Olympics. At the age of 38, Takacs won the Gold Medal and set a new world record in pistol shooting. Four years later, Takacs won the Gold Medal again at the 1952 Helsinki Olympics. Takacs – a man with the mental toughness to bounce back from anything.

Winners in every field have a special trait that helps them become unstoppable. A special characteristic that allows them to survive major setbacks on the road to success. Winners recover QUICKLY. Bouncing back is not enough. Winners bounce back QUICKLY. They take their hit, they experience their setback, they have the wind taken out of their sails, but they immediately recover. Right away they FORCE themselves to look at the bright side of things – ANY bright side, and they say to themselves," That's OK. There is always a way. I will find a way." They dust themselves off, and pick up where they left off. The reason quick recovery is important is that if you recover quickly, you don't lose your momentum and your drive. Takacs recovered in only one month. If he had wallowed in his misery, if he had stayed "under the circumstances," if he had played the martyr, and felt sorry for himself much longer, he would have lost his mental edge – his "eye of the tiger" and he never would have been able to come back.

When a boxer gets knocked down, he has ten seconds to get back up. If he gets up in eleven seconds, he loses the fight. Remember that next time you get knocked down.

Takacs definitely had a right to feel sorry for himself. He had a right to stay depressed and to ask himself "Why me?" for the rest of his life. He had the right to act like a mediocre man.

Takacs could have let his terrible accident cause him to become permanently discouraged, to take up heavy drinking, to quit on life altogether, and maybe even to end his own life. He could have acted like a loser.

But Takacs made the DECISION to dig deep inside and to find a solution. To pick himself up and to learn to shoot all over again. Winners always search for a solution. Losers always search for an escape.

Next time you get knocked down, DECIDE you will act like a winner. DECIDE to act like Takacs. Get up quickly, take action, and astound the world!

Arunima Sinha, the First Amputee to climb Mount Everest:

In 2011, twenty four year old Arunima Sinha was thrown off a moving train by thugs for refusing to hand over the gold chain she was wearing. She lost her left leg when a train went over it. While dealing with pitying murmurs of, "Who will marry you now," and the absurd conspiracy theories that followed, she made a decision. She would climb Mount Everest. In 2013 she did just that, becoming the world's first female amputee, and the first Indian amputee, to achieve this feat. Earlier this year she was awarded the Padmashri, the fourth highest civilian award in India.

This May marks the second anniversary of her reaching Everest's summit. In honour of this phenomenal accomplishment, Arunima Sinha remembered about that ill-fated train trip, the hell that followed, why she decided to climb Everest and how it is in the worst tragedies that the human spirit learns to soar.

Success is only a matter of Cause and Effect.

I failed in 10th standard
– Sachin Tendulkar

Education drop out and initially
a key board player – AR Rahman

At the age of 25, I was a bus conductor
– Rajnikanth

I didn't even complete my university
education – Bill Gates

I worked in a petrol pump
– Dhirubhai Ambani

I slept on bench and borrowed Rs.20
every day from a friend to travel
to film city – Shah Rukh Khan

The price of success must be paid in fill, in advance.

Success is not in the profession, it is in the person. They were all lost but not defeated. They bounced back. Success is possible for you also, but then you should believe in attaining it firmly. Believe in yourself; believe in God. People may say **GOD IS NOWHERE** but let us convert that negative statement into positive - **GOD IS NOW HERE**.

Some people dream of success, while others wake up and work hard at it.

People are frozen in their comfort zones, and they are in the same jobs, like bees making honey, because they think it is the most secure job in the world. They don't want to take any risks in life. They are so comfortable in comfort zones that they do not even want to try.

Success comes to you when you move from comfort zone to effort zone.

There was a very cautious man who never laughed or played; he never risked, he never tried. He never sang or prayed. And when he one day passed away, his insurance was denied. For since he never lived they claimed he never died.

All these successful people were failures; they failed several times, but were never defeated. If we fall, fall like a seed to germinate and not like a leaf to die.

But we have some common excuses:

I am unlucky

I'm born under the wrong stars

I'm not good looking

I don't have contacts

I don't have enough money

The economy is bad

If only I had the opportunity

If only I didn't have a family

I lack Brain

I am Too Old / Young.

DON'T GIVE UP

But my health is not good remedies:

1. Refuse to talk about your health
2. Refuse to worry about your health
3. Be genuinely graceful that your health is as good as it is
4. Remind yourself often-It is better to wear out than rust out

I lack brains - remedies:

1. Never underestimate your own intelligence and never overestimate the intelligence of others.
2. My attitude is more important than my intelligence - remind yourself.
3. Ability to think is of much greater value than the ability to memorize facts

I am too old - remedies:

1. Look at your present age positively.
2. Compute how much productive time you have left.
3. Invest future time in doing what you really want to do

I am unlucky remedies:

1. Accept the law of cause and effect.
2. Don't be a wishful thinker

Either we have Reasons or Results

Every king was a crying baby once upon a time. Sachin was a crying baby; every giant tree was once upon a time a seed or sapling, every great building was once a drawing, a plan on the wall. It is not what you are now or from where you came; the most important part is where are you going from here. All those extraordinary people were once very ordinary.

So what is the difference between ordinary and extra ordinary people? What made them change into extraordinary from the ordinary? There is a small difference between them. Successful people have done something extra.

Everybody in the world wants to become somebody. Yes. It does not matter whether you are a petrol pump attendant, a small actor on TV, newspaper vendor, teacher, farmer, village boy, businessman, college dropout, hotel owner etc. But does everybody become somebody? No, why? Because someone is stopping your from becoming somebody. Who is stopping us to become somebody?

Look at the above missile, it has got enormous power. However, it is struck on the launching pad. It is tied with chains. If the missile has to hit the target, first of all we need to cut the chains. Even after cutting the chains, it will not hit the target, you have to ignite it. Ignition is required. In life we might have been tied down with lots of chains. If you remove the chains, your life will not be better; you need to take action to go forward.

This missile can go up even with the chains tied on, if you fire it; it has got that much power, but then it will not hit the target, and it may crash somewhere in the ocean. In life also you may go and hit the target, but with chains like poor habits, laziness, lack of knowledge, bad behaviour, negative attitude, indecent character etc. you may also crash land. Most people climb up the ladder of success very quickly, but then they realize that ladder was leaning on the wrong wall.

You have been tied down with lots of chains. What are your chains? May be parents, husband, wife, lack of education, lack of knowledge, lack of communication, poor habits, negative thinking, lack of confidence, family background, environment, past experience, etc. might have played a major role in moulding what you are now. First of all you need to identify what are your chains that hold you back and then it is important to cut all those chains that affect your life.

A Professor in a college, a real genius had an unmatchable knowledge of business management. Everybody admired his knowledge and wondered at the depth of his information. But he rarely turned up for his classes. Whenever he came, he taught for a few minutes and then pushed off. Those who did assignments under him complained that he never checked them on time and usually made then wait for assessments.

He had enormous talent. He had extraordinary knowledge. But he had enormous appetite for laziness and extraordinary lackadaisical approach. He just couldn't use his potential. He also was a failure. And worse, he knew it. And he didn't want to change it. He was a sophisticated failure. He was born to win but destined to live an ordinary life.

You are where you are and what you are because of yourself, and not because of anyone else.

The first chain is, you are all conditioned or programmed for mediocrity. You think that you were born to live average life. In the early stages of your life, your parents, grandparents, brothers, sisters, peers, surroundings, have bombarded with lots of "should nots" and "cannots". And you are the victims of that negative programming.

When an elephant is small, it is tied up with big chain. It starts struggling to get away from that chain and keeps on trying for a long time. Then it becomes conditioned and stops trying. Then after that, it is tied up with a chain of lesser strength to a small tree. If the elephant were to try once again, it could easily break that chain and could even uproot the tree. But it has already been conditioned that it is impossible to detach the chain. You have grown like an elephant. You now have the strength. You don't know your strength. Elephants want freedom. You also want freedom. Future Freedom, Financial Freedom. Break the chain and go forward.

A rat was put in a closed room and some food was kept inside. The moment it starts eating the food, an electric shock is given to the rat and it retreats. After a few attempts, the rat is left with no choice but to quit. Because every time it attempts to have the food, the electric shock is there. The scientists then changed the scenario and put more attractive food in the room, and the electric shock was also removed. But the rat did not try at all. Why, because it knows if it tries, it will die. Finally the rat died, not because of electric shock but because of starvation. One more try could have saved its life.

An experiment was done with five monkeys. They were locked in a room and a bunch of bananas was kept on the top of a ladder in the middle of the room. When one of the monkeys went up the ladder to take a banana, the scientists soaked the rest of the monkeys with cold water. So the other four monkeys started beating the one who climbed up the ladder. Each and every time a monkey climbed up the ladder, the others beat up the one climbing the ladder. This was continued with all five monkeys, one by one; all of them experienced the cold water spray.

After some time, no monkey dared go up the ladder regardless of the temptation. Scientists then decided to substitute one of the monkeys with a new monkey. The first thing this new monkey did was to go up the ladder. Immediately the other monkeys beat him up. After several beatings, the new member learned not to climb the ladder even though it never knew why. But now the scientists stopped spraying cold water on the other monkeys. A second monkey was substituted and the same occurred. The first monkey participated in the beating of the second monkey. A third monkey was changed and the same behaviour was repeated. The fourth was substituted and the beating was repeated and finally the fifth monkey was replaced.

What was left was a group of five monkeys that even though never received a cold shower, continued to beat up any monkey who attempted to climb the ladder. This is a glaring example of programming of our mind.

It was a common belief that running the four-minute mile is impossible for an athlete to do, and attempting to do so was dangerous to one's health. The belief was there till Roger Bannister from England crossed that barrier on 6th May 1954. The significant fact is that after breaking this four minute mile barrier, many college students broken the feat. What happened there, it was the mindset of the people that was broken by Bannister.

STORY:

> Once there was a king who received a gift of two magnificent falcons from Arabia. They were peregrine falcons, the most beautiful birds he had ever seen. He gave the precious birds to his head falconer to be trained. Months passed by and one day the head falconer informed the king that though one of the falcons was flying majestically, soaring high in the sky, the other bird had not moved from its branch since the day it had arrived.
>
> The king summoned healers and sorcerers from all the land to tend to the falcon, but no one could make the bird fly. He presented the task to the member of his court, but the next day, the king saw through the palace window that the bird had still not moved from its perch. Having tried everything else, the king thought to himself, "May be I need someone more familiar with the countryside to understand the nature of this problem." So he cried out to his court, "Go and get a farmer."
>
> In the morning, the king was thrilled to see the falcon soaring high above the palace gardens. He said to his court, "Bring me the doer of this miracle." The court quickly located the farmer, who came and stood before the king. The king asked him, "How did you make the falcon fly?" With his head bowed, the farmer said to the king, " It was very easy, your highness. I simply cut the branch where the bird was sitting."

You are made to fly - to realize your incredible potential as human beings. But instead of doing that, you sit on your branches, clinging to the things that are familiar to you. The possibilities are endless, but for most of you, they remain undiscovered. You conform to the familiar, the comfortable, the mundane. So for the most part, your lives are mediocre instead of exciting, thrilling and fulfilling. So learn to destroy the branch of fear you cling to and free yourselves for the glory of flight.

The second chain is fear of failure and criticism. What will happen if you fail while trying? This stops many people from doing something new. They worry a lot about what's going to happen. What will happen if that fear is realized? What is the best possible outcome for you, if you acted in spite of your fears?

If somebody is criticizing you, it means they think that you are better than them. They don't want you to grow. **See the source of their criticism.** Who is criticizing you, what authority do they have to criticize you? What are their motives of criticism? What accuracy is there in that criticism? Check all that and say big thanks to them. At least somebody is there to bring up your weaknesses to you. Great people build monuments from the bricks that are thrown at them by critics.

Worry is a misuse of Imagination

The third chain is no clear cut Goal. What is your goal? Every person in the world devotes too much time to think about their future and their present situation in life. Whether it is their family life, social life, financial life or physical life, the first step to doing that is to set goals. However, many people set goals and most of them are practically incapable of following through with it. Sometimes even setting goals at all is the hardest part of accomplishing anything. We all set New Year resolutions every year, which lasts for only a few days.

By setting goals and measuring your achievement from time to time, you will be able to see what you have done and what you are capable of doing. The process of achieving goals and seeing this achievement gives you the confidence and a belief in yourself that you need to be able to achieve higher and more difficult goals. We have a separate chapter dedicated to goal setting, which will help you to set a goal, visualise it and achieve it.

The fourth chain is your lack of know how. You don't have the right kind of recipe for success. All successful people have left some clues to their recipe for success. Suppose your wife or mother knows how to prepare the best pizza and you want to make the same pizza, you don't have to reinvent. What you have to do is to copy the recipe. If you do it the same way your mother or wife made that pizza, you can also make it, may be initially it will not be as good. But with couple of experiments, your pizza might even be better than theirs. So if you want to succeed in any area, you have to find out the successful people in that area and ask for their recipe. Copy it, don't waste time in reinventing.

The last chain is your lack of resources. You need people to complete your task. You have to delegate some jobs. Never do a job which others can do for you. You do what you have to do for your betterment, upward career growth and spend time with your family. Leave all petty things to other people. If you really want to be successful, you must develop a good team. You must find a way to get your vision seen, implemented and contributed to by others. You see the big picture, but you also need others to help make your big picture a reality.

Intelligent delegation is one of a leader's basic duties. Never do anything yourself that someone else can do for you as well or better. Delegation begins by determining all the tasks that must be performed to reach your organisation's goals. Then select the individual or individuals best qualified to handle each duty and empower them to do it. Finally, check results regularly to make sure the productivity goals you've set are being reached or surpassed.

DO YOU BELIEVE?

Do you believe that there is something you could specifically do in the next two weeks that would make your personal life, your family life or your business life **WORSE**? Yes or No?

Do you believe that there is something you could specifically do in the next two weeks that would make your personal life, your family life or your business life **BETTER**? Yes or No?

Do you believe that every choice has an end result? Yes or No?

So you have agreed that you don't care how good or bad your past has been. You don't care how difficult your circumstances are at this precise moment. There is something you can do right now that will make your future either better or worse...and the choice is yours. **A stone that is fit for the wall will not be left on the road for long time.** Be a big stone that others can't move. If you are a small stone, people will kick often.

Difficulties, failures and obstacles would be powerless if you follow the success principles.

TEN COMMANDMENTS OF SUCCESS:

1.	TALK TO PEOPLE	There is nothing as nice as a cheerful greeting
2.	SMILE	It takes 72 muscles to frown and only 14 to smile
3.	CALL PEOPLE BY THEIR NAMES	Everyone is pleased when you remember their name.
4.	BE FRIENDLY AND HELPFUL	And others will respond in like manner
5.	SPEAK AND ACT	As if everything you do were genuine pleasure
6.	BE GENUINE	Interested in people
7.	BE GENEROUS	With praise
8.	BE CONSIDERATE	It will be appreciated
9.	BE THOUGHTFUL	Of the opinions of others
10.	BE WILLING	To give service

FEED YOUR MIND WITH SUCCESS:

Today everything can be predicted in life. Development of Science and Technology can predict many things. It can predict when it will rain, it can predict when there will be flood, it can predict many things. But there is one thing that cannot be predicted, and whoever predicted went wrong. What is that?

It is the potential of human being. A young boy was labelled by a Teacher as he was too stupid to learn anything. He will never become anything and that boy was fired from school. And he became Thomas Alva Edison.

Her doctor told she would never walk again,' but she didn't listen him. So she ran. And that young American black girl affected with polio proved the doctor wrong. She won three gold medals, in the 100- and 200-meter individual events and the 4 x 100-meter relay at the 1960 Summer Olympics in Rome, Italy. Wilma Rudolph was acclaimed the fastest woman in the world in the 1960s and became the first American woman to win three gold medals in a single Olympic Games.

A young man was rejected by 'All India Radio' when he applied at the radio network after finishing his university education. But he became the Superstar of Bollywood. He is Amitabh Bhachhan.

All the prediction about human beings are proved wrong. But I can predict your life. What you will become after 5 years?

There is a popular quote going around at the moment – the person you will be in 5 years is based on the books you read, the thoughts you think, the food you eat, the people you hang around from today. This is quite true but it applies to everything as well. The person you will be in the future is based on **EVERYTHING YOU DO TODAY**. The people you hang around with but more so the people you listen to, the opinions you believe. The books you read or the videos you watch all the information you take on positive or negative will affect your future. The work outs you do or don't do that will show up in the future. The food you eat today will affect your future on a visual and energy level. The same is true with your THOUGHTS and INFORMATION. **What you FEED YOUR MIND will SHAPE YOUR FUTURE.**

Commit to feed your mind with successful thoughts and surround yourself with those who have the same ambition. It doesn't matter where you get information from you may read, you may get it from videos, magazines – it doesn't matter. Just make sure you keep **FEEDING YOUR MIND EVERYDAY.**

The fight of TWO WOLVES WITHIN YOU. A master is teaching his disciple about life: "A fight is going on inside me," Disciple said to the Master. "It is a terrible fight and it is between two wolves. One is evil–he is anger, envy, sorrow, regret, greed, arrogance, self-pity, guilt, resentment, inferiority, lies, false pride, superiority, and ego."

He continued, "The other is good – he is joy, peace, love, hope, serenity, humility, kindness, benevolence, empathy, generosity, truth, compassion, and faith. The same fight is going on inside you–and inside every other person, too."

The disciple thought about it for a minute and then asked the master: "Which wolf will win?"

The master simply replied, **"The one you feed."**

If you don't **FEED YOUR MIND WITH SUCCESS, it will ROT with MEDIOCRITY**. What you do every day will dictate your future. **YOUR ACTIONS WILL EQUAL YOUR RESULTS**. Whatever you add to "I AM," this is what you become. I am RICH, I am PASSIONATE. I AM ENTHUSIASTIC. I AM STRONG. I AM COURAGEOUS. I AM POWERFUL.

SECRETS OF SUCCESS:

Have you ever heard of the "Secrets of Success"? The so-called "Secrets" are mostly common sense and hard work. We all know these "secrets". We just have to apply them and use them consistently.

Secret-1 People: Dealing with people can be hard, but we all know we must be courteous and professional. You need to accept the fact that you cannot please everybody. When you come across one of these people you cannot please no matter what you do, just deal with them firmly, but courteously and professionally. – Now no more a "secret".

Secret-2 Passion: We all know that we need to like what we do in order to be really successful at all. If you are interested in pets, do not start a business dealing with cars, there will be many times when we will need our passion to get us through. Now no more a "secret".

Secret-3 Customer-Service: Another "secret" is to treat the customer with respect and courtesy. It will not be easy to deal with difficult customers this way, but it can be done. Anybody can cool down the nastiest customers by a continuing campaign of courtesy, politeness and professionalism. Now no more a 'secret'

Secret-4 Promotion: To build a business, people must know that you and your business exist. Advertising, promotion and networking are how this is done. Set up a promotion schedule and stick with it. Be consistent. This may get tedious at times, but it must be done.

Secret-5 Hard work: Despite what many people have said, it is not easy to "get rich overnight" and "make thousands a week, while doing nothing" just doesn't happen. To be successful you will need to work and word hard. This is where passion for your work comes in.

Secret-6 **Commitment:** Expanding on the hard work "secret", you will need to make a commitment to success. You must be willing to make sacrifices and work long hours. This will not happen overnight, it could take years. Be prepared for years of frustration, hard work, ups and downs, and dealing with good and bad people, rejections and everything else that comes along with building of a business or a career.

Secret-7 **Pride:** Take pride in your work. Your work and your business will be a reflection of you. Build your reputation for a solid foundation of success. Be true to yourself and your business.

Secret-8 **Goals:** Be aware of what you want and how you want to get it. Do not go blindly into business without some planning of your goals and accomplishments. Use short term goals to eventually reach your long term ultimate goal of life.

TIPS FOR MAKING LIFE SUCCESSFUL:

1. Take a 45 Minute Walk Every Day and While You Walk, Smile.
2. Sit in Silence for at Least 10 Minutes Each Day.
3. Sleep for 7 Hours.
4. Live With The 3 Es - Energy, Enthusiasm, And Empathy.
5. Play more useful Games.
6. Read more Books than You Did last year.
7. Make Time to Practice Meditation, Yoga, and Prayer. They Provide Us with Daily Fuel For Our Busy Lives.
8. Spend Time With People Over The Age of 70 & Under The Age Of 6.
9. Dream More While You Are Awake.
10. Eat More Foods That Grow On Trees And Plants And Eat Less Food That Is Manufactured In Plants.
11. Drink Plenty of Water.
12. Try To Make At Least Three People Smile Each Day.
13. Don't Waste Your Precious Energy On Gossip.

14. Forget Issues Of The Past. Don't Remind Your Partner With Their Mistakes Of The Past. That Will Ruin Your Present Happiness.
15. Don't Have Negative Thoughts Over Things You Cannot Control. Instead Invest Your Energy in The Positive Present Moment.
16. Realize That Life Is A School And You Are Here To Learn. Problems Are Simply Part Of The Curriculum That Appear And Fade Away Like Algebra Class But The Lessons You Learn Will Last A Lifetime.
17. Eat Breakfast Like A King, Lunch Like A Prince And Dinner Like A Beggar.
18. Smile And Laugh More.
19. Life Is Too Short To Waste Time Hating Anyone. Don't Hate Others.
20. Don't Take Yourself So Seriously. No One Else Does.
21. You Don't Have To Win Every Argument. Agree To Disagree.
22. Make Peace With Your Past So It Won't Spoil The Present.
23. Don't Compare Your Life To Others'. You Have No Idea What Their Journey Is All About. Don't Compare Your Partner With Others.
24. No One Is In Charge Of Your Happiness Except You.
25. Forgive Everyone For Everything.
26. What Other People Think Of You Is None Of Your Business.
27. GOD ! Heals Everything.
28. However Good Or Bad A Situation Is, It Will Change.
29. Your Job Won't Take Care Of You When You Are Sick. Your Friends Will. Stay In Touch.
30. Get Rid Of Anything That Isn't Useful, Beautiful Or Joyful.
31. Envy Is A Waste Of Time. You Already Have All You Need.
32. The Best Is Yet To Come.
33. No Matter How You Feel, Get Up, Dress Up And Show Up.
34. Do The Right Thing!
35. Call Your Family Often.
36. Your Inner Most Is Always Happy. So Be Happy.
37. Each Day Give Something Good To Others.
38. Don't Over Do. Keep Your Limits.
39. When You Awake Alive In The Morning, Thank GOD For It.

Success is never final just like failure is never fatal

WHAT IS YOUR CHANCE OF SUCCESS?

Assessing your chance of success makes you aware of your strengths and weaknesses. It then becomes possible to correct them before they get a hold of you and stop you from making the best of yourselves. Here is a test you can try on yourself. Answer **YES** or **NO** to the questions before turning to the key at the end of this questionnaire.

1. Do you know what you want to do? Do you have a definite ambition in mind?
2. Is what you want to do really and truly suitable to your capabilities so that it lies within a reasonable possibility of achievement?
3. Have you worked out a plan of progress so that you know, step by step, how to set about achieving your goal?
4. Have you obtained or are you in the process of obtaining, the necessary training and qualifications for fulfilling your ambition?
5. Are you in the habit of taking the utmost advantage of outside interests and activities, such as lectures and extra classes, likely to further your knowledge, add to your experience and put you in touch with useful and helpful people?
6. What about your social life? Is it reasonably easy for you to meet people and talk to them and get along with them?
7. Do you watch out for any irritating mannerisms of speech and habits in yourself and consciously correct them?
8. Are you quick at spotting opportunities for advancement and taking advantage of them?
9. Would you take the initiative and go at it alone if this meant taking a risk?
10. Are you prepared to change jobs and move around in the interest of promotion?
11. Do you listen when people are talking and pay attention and remember what is useful and important?

12. Do you ask intelligent questions, make sensible comments and put forward useful ideas?
13. Do you weigh up all the merits and setbacks and make up your own mind?
14. Can you distinguish between constructive criticism, which is helpful and often encouraging and destructive criticism, which is often mischievous and may even be malicious?
15. Can you work on your own without supervision?
16. Can you also obey orders, follow instructions, and bear to be briefed, shown how and corrected, without becoming disagreeable?
17. Can you stick to a job until you finish it even when it is hard, unpleasant or monotonous?
18. Do you take pride in the standard of your work and welcome responsibility as an opportunity to show what you can do?
19. Are difficulties and problems a challenge to spur you on to more effect?
20. Are you far too busy finding and examining the cause of a failure to allow it to depress you for long?

Count five marks for every YES. A score of **70+ is good and 60 to 70 are satisfactory. 50 to 60 are only fair. Under 50 is poor**. Don't get agitated even if you get below 50. It shows only that you need to work on it more.

"You know what you are,
but you don't know what you can become"

VITAL's Success Formula*

(Follow these 10 steps to achieve your dreams)

1. **Decide what you want**
   (If you don't have a dream, how will it come true?)
2. **Write it down and be specific**
   (Don't just say that you want to be rich)
3. **Read your goals three times daily**
   (Once in the morning, afternoon, again before you go to bed)
4. **Set a deadline**
   (If you set a date, you will not postpone it)
5. **Think of it often**
   (Motivate yourself by envisioning your success often)
6. **Dream and Imagine**
   (Use power of positive visualization. See yourself enjoying it)
7. **Develop a plan of action**
   (Plan your work, and then work on your plan)
8. **Do three things every day towards the goal**
   (Three things done consistently is better than ten things done inconsistently)
9. **Stay positive**
   (Make self-motivation as routine as bathing)
10. **Act like you have already achieved it**
    (Act your way into a new way of thinking, and think your way into a new way of acting)

***VITAL is my training organisation "VITAL TRAINING"**

HAPPINESS

Let us begin with an insightful story:

"I need your help, or I will go mad. I am in a dire state of unhappiness. My wife, my children, my in-laws and I stay together in a single room. So our nerves are on edge, we yell and scream at one another. The room is a hell." A disciple complained to his Master. Do you promise to do whatever I tell you? Said the Master gravely. "I swear I shall do anything. "Well. How many animals do you have?" "A cow, a goat and six hens." "Take them all into the room with you. Then come back after a week".

The disciple was appalled. But he had promised to obey! So he took the animals in. A week later he came back, a pitiable figure moaning, "I am nervous wreck. The dirt! The stench! The noise! We are all on the verge of madness!" "Go back, "said the Master, "and put the animals out. The man ran all the way home. And came back the following day, his eyes sparkling with joy. "How sweet life is! The animals are out. The home is a paradise so quiet and clean and roomy."

There are three things to remember about happiness:

1. **Happiness is Important**
2. **Happiness is Desirable**
3. **Happiness is Possible**

Happiness is a place between too little and too much. Happiness is a state of mind and it can be achieved by anyone. It is simply waiting for you. It is an achievement that you can claim as your own. You are not born happy, but rather you develop your capacity for bringing happiness in your life. Happiness is only within your reach but first you have to admit that it is a definite possibility. Once you become aware of that possibility, you can reorganize your thinking and work towards attaining happiness. You need to prepare yourself for happiness just as you would prepare for any possible occurrence. Happiness breeds happiness. You need to start by being ready to accept it. How can you prepare yourself? One way is to remove your barriers against happiness.

Achieving happiness with all the comforts is the core objective of one's life, irrespective of race, gender, status, education, position, knowledge, age etc. No matter what your past circumstances have been, no matter what your present conditions are, happiness is possible for you. You can learn to develop it. Through the power of truth, there is wealth. Through the power of peace, there is health. Together they provide happiness. Awareness and application of spiritual truths are the true source of happiness. The warmth and comfort of happiness is hidden within the self. For many, self-progress and personal transformation is the keys to happiness. Happiness of mind is a state of peace in which there is no upheaval, no violence.

Do you want to know the short cut to making yourself happy?

Make someone else happy.

REQUIREMENTS FOR BRINGING HAPPINESS:

1. **Take an interest in the world around you.** Get out and see the world. It is full of great people to associate with. Enjoy the funny things that happen. Participate in various social activities and you will find immense pleasure in your life. Get mixed with people.
2. **Have a willingness to work intensely.** Doing the work you enjoy is a key to happiness, success and prosperity. The work you enjoy is the best guarantee you can find for a long, happy and healthy life. Do what you love or love what you do.

3. **Appreciate your leisure time.** Utilize your leisure time effectively to revitalize your energy and enjoy it fully.
4. **Understand solitude in a better way.** In loneliness only you can dream. Utilize it fully and have a big dream. Meditate, introspect and relax totally.
5. **List out your past achievements:** You may have much more achievements in your life than you think. List out your positive qualities, victories and all achievements made till this moment. Take a piece of paper and write them down. These blessings may be readily visible to you; they may be spiritual, physical, social, financial, or emotional in nature. Do not eliminate anything and list everything, no matter how small of a personal triumph it was. Knowing them will help you to build your self-esteem and a high level of self-esteem is needed for happiness.
6. **List your anticipations that you feel are attainable:** Anticipation can play a big part in your happiness. Looking forward and planning for the future are attributes of a happy person.
7. **Learn to sharpen and develop your observation:** Don't go through life as if you have dull senses. Life is to be seen, felt, tasted, smelled and heard.
8. **Take time to enjoy your life:** Don't hurry through your life. Take time out to enjoy the world around you.
9. **Replace fear in your life with happiness:** Fears are common to us all, but we do not need to hang on to them.

Some characteristics of Happy people

Happy people are thoughtful people

Happy people are considerate people

Happy people have better health

Happy people show their age less

Happy people like themselves

Happy people are liked by others

Happy people are successful in what they do

The good we do today becomes the happiness of tomorrow.

Secret of happiness

Smile without mocking Help without taking Give without expecting

Love without suspecting Speak without hurting Compete without fighting Work without straining Rest without lazing

Plan without scheming

Act without wavering Think without worrying Thank without thinking

Happiness is a wonderful commodity, the more you give, the more you have.

Today once again I will choose happiness. **When you get up in the morning, you have two choices, either to be happy or to be unhappy. "The choice is entirely yours".**

The Be-happy attitude says "I need your help, I can't do it alone"!

The way to handle your area of poverty is to say, "I need help". There's always somebody ready to help you. Ask for help. Admit your need for help, it is not easy, but it is essential. Happiness comes when you admit where you are lacking and where you have a need. We are reluctant to admit to our needs because we are afraid that people might really reject us. We are afraid of public embarrassment.

Life's rule - Ask for what you want and if you won't get it, you won't lose, but it is a break-even. It is a rejection of the request by the other person and not their rejection of you. The other person's right to say 'NO' is valid.

The Be-happy attitude says, "I am Sorry":

When you learn to make this confession, you will find happiness, because you will discover the miracle working power of a honest person. You and I can become free when we admit we have been or done wrong. Instead of an ego trip, we are on an integrity - trip the road to real happiness. So learn to say 'Sorry'.

Nobody else can make you happy and nobody else can make you unhappy. The real happiness lies within.

FEELING REJECTED? NEGLECTED?

Many a times you may have thought that you were being rejected from something good, you were in fact being redirected to something better. You cannot control everything. Sometimes you just need to relax and have faith that things will work out for the good. Because sometimes the truths you cannot change, end up changing you and helping you grow. It is crazy how you always end up where you were meant to be – how even the most tragic and stressful situations eventually teach you important lessons that you never dreamed you were going to learn. Remember, often when things are falling apart, they are actually falling into place.

The first step is to live the life you want.
The second step is leaving the life you don't want.

Making a big life change is pretty scary. But you know what is even scarier? Regret. Vision without action is a day dream, and action without vision is a nightmare. Your heart is free, have the courage to follow it.

Without pain, there will be no change. But remember, pain, just like everything in life, is meant to be learned from and then released. One of the hardest decisions you will ever face in life is choosing whether to walk away or take another step forward. If you catch yourself in a cycle of trying to change someone, or defending yourself against someone who is trying to change you, walk away. But if you are pursuing a dream, take another step. And don't forget that sometimes this step will involve modifying your dream, or planning a new one – it is OK to change your mind or have more than one dream.

Some Tips:

You have to take care of yourself first:

Before making new friends, you have to become your own friend. Before correcting others, you have to correct yourself. Before making others happy, you have to make yourself happy. It is not called selfishness, it is called personal development. Once you balance yourself, you can balance the world around you.

Lok kya kahenge or What will people say syndrome is the biggest problem in life:

One of the greatest form of freedom is truly not caring what everyone else thinks of you. As long as you are worried about what others think of you, you will be owned by them. Only when you require no approval from anyone but yourself, can you own yourself.

The only thing you can absolutely control is how you react to things that are out of your control:

The more you can adapt to the situations in life, the more powerful your highs will be and the more quickly you will be able to bounce back from the lows in your life. Put most simply; being at peace means being in a state of complete acceptance of all that is, right here, right now.

Some people will lie to you:

Remember, an honest enemy is better than a friend who lies. Pay less attention to what people say, and more attention to what they do. Their actions will show you the truth, which will help you to measure the true quality of your relationship in the long-run.

If you concentrate on what you don't have, you will never have enough:

If you are thankful for what you do have, you will end up having even more; Happiness resides not in possessions and gold, happiness dwells in the soul. Abundance is not about how much you have, it is how you feel about what you have. When you take things for granted, your happiness gets taken away.

Have you failed in the past?

But don't judge yourself by your past, you don't live there anymore. Just because you are not where you want to be today doesn't mean you won't be there someday. You can turn it all around in the blink of an eye by making a simple choice; to stand back up – to try again, to love again, to live again, and to dream again.

Everything is going to be alright; may be not today, but eventually:

There will be times when it seems like everything that could possibly go wrong is going wrong. And you might feel like you will be stuck in this rut forever, but you won't. Sure the sun stops shining sometimes, and you may get a huge thunderstorm or two but eventually the sun will come out. Sometimes it's just a matter of staying as positive as possible in order to make it to see the sunshine break through the clouds again.

LOVE YOURSELF:

Self-love means something different for each person, because we all have many different ways to show that we love ourselves. The real question is why should we even care?

Self-love is important to living well. It influences who you pick for a mate, the image you project at work, and how you cope with the problems in your life. It is so important to your welfare that I want you to know how to bring more of it into your life. What is self-love then? Is it something you can buy in a beauty shop or a new set of clothing? Can you get more of it by reading something inspirational? Or can a new relationship make you love yourself more? The answer to all these questions is NO. Although they feel good and are gratifying, you can't grow in self-love through these types of activities. Self-love is not simply a state of feeling good. Self-love is a state of appreciation of oneself that grows from actions that support our physical, psychological and spiritual growth. Self-love is dynamic; it grows by actions that mature us. When we act in ways that expand self-love in us, we begin to accept our weaknesses as well as our strengths much better, have less need to explain away our shortcomings, have compassion for ourselves as human beings struggling to find personal meaning, are more centred in our life purpose and values and expect living fulfilment through our own efforts.

Prescription for Self-Love:

- Practice good care of yourself: You will love yourself more, when you take better care of your basic needs and habits. People high in self-love nourish themselves daily through healthy activities, like nutrition, exercise, proper sleep, intimacy and healthy social interactions.
- Protect yourself from negative people: Bring the right people into your life. There is not enough time in your life to waste on people who want to take away the shine on your face.
- Find your happy place: Think of a place that makes it simple to just be. That means being able to sit quietly and embrace the moment.

Not thinking about what is due at work or what bills need to be paid. Connect with yourself and one of the easiest places to do that is your happy place.

- Do something you are good at: If this is not the ultimate self-esteem booster, I don't know what is? Self-esteem and self-love often go hand in hand, and participating in a hobby you are good at will not only boost your endorphins, but will bring out the best version of you. If you love to sing, then sing; if you love to play cricket; go and play.

DO YOURSELF EVERYDAY:

Focus on Self:

Note down Daily basis analysis in a diary before going to bed:

"3 things you did good" and "2 things you did bad"

As a

Contributor in the organization

Son/Daughter

Brother/Sister

Spouse/Partner

Parent

Relative/Friend

Citizen

RULES FOR MAKING EVERY DAY A GREAT DAY:

1. Think that good things will happen
2. Express gratitude to a loved one.
3. Be patient with an annoying person.
4. Do something special for yourself.
5. Reach out to someone who needs comfort.
6. Focus deeply on each moment.
7. Learn from a mistake
8. Look closely at a flower or tree that you haven't notice before.
9. Smile

GOAL

(GETTING ORGANISED ABOUT LIFE)

Be honest and ask these critical thinking questions to yourself:

1. All successful people have goals. Do you have goals?
2. "Are my habits, behaviour and actions congruent with the goal I have for my life?
3. Why do most people sleep so much?

Those who rise with the sun have one thing in common. They all have a purpose that fans the flames of their inner potential. They are driven by their priorities. And given their enthusiasm, and love for what they are doing in their lives, such people live in the moment. Their attention is fully and completely given to the task at hand.

Goal means Getting Organised About Life. When you have a goal, you will become organized. You can also say a goal is nothing but vision broken into pieces. Your goal may be hourly, daily, weekly, monthly or yearly, which ultimately leads to a vision.

Many people have dreams, but they do not really know where they want to go. If you ask most people, what is their one major objective in life, they would probably give you a vague answer, such as, I want to be successful, be happy, make a good living, and that is it. They are all wishes and none of them are clear goals. Harvard University had conducted a research through a questionnaire to outgoing graduates on goals. It was found that 90% students had no goals. 10% students had some goals and out of which only 3% students had SMART - Specific, Measurable, Achievable, Realistic and Time bound goals in writing.

To achieve effective goals, it must be written out. It must be stamped upon your mind by repetition. Write it out and paste it on the mirror. You must make big plans. A person with dynamic purpose is a person who is on fire.

Not all goals are achieved.
But noting is achieved without a goal.

WHAT IS 'SMART' GOAL?

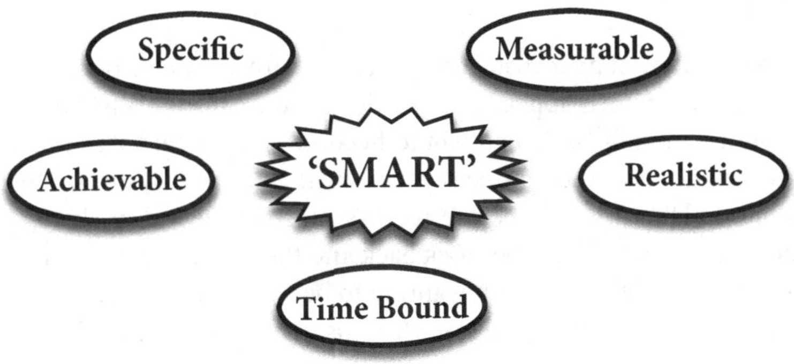

SPECIFIC:

You have to be very specific when you set a goal. If you go to a train station and ask for ticket to Maharashtra, you will not get one. You have to ask for a specific station, say Andheri, Mumbai Central etc. An example of a good specific goal is the need to make 20 phone calls today or write 10 emails. Nothing can be more specific than this. But is this is an example of a goal or a task? It is a task not a goal. Goals are dreams; tasks are the things you have to do. Do not demean your dreams by equating it with tasks. I want to lose some weight. This is just wishful thinking. It becomes a goal when I pin myself down to "I will lose 10 Kilos in 90 days".

MEASURABLE:

Dreams are not measurable; tasks are. To become a world class athlete or to write a book or win a marathon are dreams that are not measurable. The journey to achieve your dreams is as enjoyable as, in fact even more enjoyable than achieving the dream. Even if you were to fail to achieve your dreams, the journey would have been exciting and would have given you a lot of happiness. If you cannot measure it, you cannot accomplish it. Measuring is a way of monitoring your progress.

ACHIEVABLE:

If the goal is achievable, it is not very inspiring in trying to go for it. These so called achievable goals are just targets that remind you of the annual performance review and the negotiations to reduce or redefine your targets. Your goals should be just enough out of reach to be challenging; but it should not be out of sight, otherwise it becomes disheartening. To win a marathon or a run is a dream while running every day for 30 minutes is a target.

REALISTIC:

Goals cannot be realistic otherwise they are just milestones. Goals are lofty dreams which appear impossible and unrealistic. Who would have thought Amitabh Bachchan would become a superstar? Was it realistic? Who would have thought Narayana Murthy and Infosys would become so big or Dhoni would be the world's most successful cricket captain? These are dreams. Turn the clock back and they would appear unrealistic, almost impossible. A person wanting to be a superstar overnight is unrealistic. A person wanting to lose 10 Kilos in a day is unrealistic.

TIME BOUND:

Dreams cannot have timelines. Following your dreams is a journey and not just about the destination, so it cannot have an expiry date. It is a continuous process. If you like playing a sport, do you plan your retirement date as well or if you like writing do you have a deadline for when you will stop? Never. Your tasks and targets have timelines, not your dreams. There should be a starting date and finishing date only for your targets.

You cannot hit the target you cannot see

In fact we do not have goals. Most of us are like donkeys, chasing carrots which our employers will never let us have. The donkey knows where it is going. We are stuck to the promise of annual raises and go through a cradle to grave employment, without knowing where we are being lead. If you don't work to fulfil your goals, someone else will use you to fulfil theirs. And this is what happens to you. You work day in and out to complete the targets set by others for a monthly pay cheque. You go on chasing the carrot throughout your life, without knowing where you are going. At the end of the day the person sitting on the cart reaches their destination and you only manage to get a bite of the carrot.

Your goals are the road maps that guide you and show you what is possible in your life.

The best time to plant a tree was 20 years ago and the second best time is today. Goal is an end towards which some efforts are required. Stephen Covey, the author of Seven Habits of Highly Effective People said the Habit No.2 is **"Begin with the end in mind".** For example as a part of your long term vision, you have to go to Bangalore. What do you need to know first; people normally say, we should have information about Bangalore, we should know the mode of transport, how many hours will it take to reach there etc. However, if you look again, it is more important that you should first know why you want to go to Bangalore. **The purpose should be clear and strong.** Then you should know when you want to reach Bangalore. Once you know these things, where you want to go, why you are going and when you will reach there, your goal is almost set.

A great message – WINNERS AND LOSERS HAVE THE SAME GOAL – Then why winners win and losers lose?

How many people have goals that they know - the where, why and when of? What next? Now you should know where you are; from where you have come is not that important. But if you know where you are and where you want to go, it will be easy to know how much distance is there, how many hours it will take, do you have an exact road map with you. Suppose you are in Ahmedabad and you want to go to Bangalore to attend an interview on a particular date. Here you can exactly calculate when to leave from Ahmedabad to reach Bangalore to attend the interview.

Now let us say you have started your journey by rail towards Bangalore on a particular date and time to reach at a particular date and time with some purpose in mind. Somewhere in between these stations, the train halted and could not go any further because there was a derailment that occurred. Now what should you do? Should you return or proceed to the destination? Definitely you should change your direction and not the destination, because your purpose is very strong. If the purpose was weak, you could have returned.

Now look at this way - when you play football, your eyes are on the goal post. The first step you take is to kick the ball. Do you think the ball will reach the goal post? No, it is not easy to hit the goal, because there are so many opponents like the forward, midfielders, defenders and then the goal keeper. It takes lot of effort to hit the goal and during 90 minutes you have to hit the goal. Here the target is fixed; you know the obstacles, the duration etc.

What are the obstacles or blocks in your life? It may be your parents, environment, teachers, peers, bosses, lack of knowledge, poor habits, laziness etc. Those who overcome all these obstacles will hit the goal. But you have certain self-defeating habits and you defend those destructive habits by indefensible logics. So what can you do? Make a list of things which you need to do or should do in your career. These are your tasks. Make them smart. Now think about your dreams, something which comes from inside you. Remember you do not find your dream, your dream finds you. Choose that dream and dedicate your all to it and you will never ever regret it in your life.

The tragedy of life is not in not achieving the goals you set, but in not having any goals to achieve.

WHY WE SET GOALS?

The sole purpose of setting a goal is to lead us on the entire journey from wish to fulfilment. When you internalize the goal setting process, your goals create a magnetic attraction that draws you towards this achievement. Writing your goals forces you to clarify and crystallize your thinking. Goals give you something to shoot for. They keep your efforts focused. Your key to personal success is having a high goal. Find the power of goals. The important thing is not where you were or where you are but where you want to reach.

Goals are powerful because they give our energy a specific focus. Goals enable you to sort out what is important in your lives and what isn't? Remember, you will not pay a price for setting goals, you will pay a price for not setting them. You can choose to get caught up in the everyday activity of your lives without feeling any real sense of purpose or you can choose to accomplish something meaningful with your lives that give you a sense of direction and self-motivation.

Unless we focus, we cannot achieve our goals. It is hard to focus and concentrate, but it is a skill that can be learned. **When you take your eyes off the goal, you will start to sink.** Everyone wants to succeed in their lives. Many of us say: "I want to succeed in my life". Well, it is the expression of a desire to succeed in life.

Having a desire is most important. But the desire alone cannot lead you to success. You must set a Goal. Your ideas must be reinforced by setting a goal, and you must prepare a plan to achieve it. Everything we see in the world around began as an idea in somebody's mind.

You must clearly know exactly what you want. Without knowing the destination there is no use of proceeding on a journey. Before you select a goal you should know what talents you possess? What are your assets and strong points? Quite possibly you may have several talents. Select one in which you can excel. On knowing and assessing your talents, you should look for an opportunity and find a way to utilize it. If you want to reach your goal, you must 'see the reaching' in your own mind before you actually arrive at your goal.

Goals are powerful because they give our energy a specific focus. Goals enable us to sort out what's important in our lives and what isn't. Goals are not cast in stone; they are changing and should be revisited and revised often. Remember, you will not have to pay a price for setting goals; you will have to pay a price for not setting them. We can choose to get caught up in the everyday activity of our lives without feeling any real sense of purpose or we can choose to accomplish something meaningful with our lives that give us a sense of direction and self- motivation.

The indispensable first step to get the things you want out of life is this – Decide what you want.

Let us take a look at few benefits of goal-setting:

- Results in clear vision of your future
- Your mind and talents are used fully
- Make better decisions
- Be more organized and effective
- Do more for our self and others
- Feel more fulfilled
- Be more enthusiastic and motivated about life
- Accomplish uncommon projects
- Focused on what we want to achieve.
- Self-confidence increases as we reach milestones along the way.
- Our outlook changes.
- No longer confused about what action to take.
- Able to prioritize our time.
- Defeat procrastination.
- See possibilities we never saw before.
- Able to accomplish more in a shorter time.
- Able to focus our energy.
- Experience a new level of success, and accomplishment

Think about a goal that you really want to achieve. Before we go through the process, make sure it's your goal and you want to achieve it for you rather than your partner or your friends or your boss. OK, when you've got a goal you need to write it down to make it clear in your head. In writing - to make them real. Goals aren't real goals until they're written down - don't be afraid to put your dreams in writing.

Goal is an end towards some specific actions you are required to take now.

So, write down your goal on a piece of paper now. It must meet all of the above SMART criteria. To find a goal, identify dissatisfactions in following areas of life. Develop goals in these areas of life.

1. Family
2. Self-improvement
3. Career and profession
4. Spiritual
5. Physical - Everyone wants it and seeks it
6. Social
7. Financial - Sometimes the most dominant drive in many people's lives.
8. Education and Knowledge
9. Gratification of appetite – Hunger and thirst for not just physical things but for mental and emotional as well.
10. Amusement – Entertainment, games, recreation and all forms of diversion.
11. Self-importance – The desire to be admired. This motive is always important in influencing others.

Some people develop financial goals because they want to make a lot of money, really fast. Mistakenly, though, some have no specific action plans; some devise action plans that are inappropriate; and, others set unrealistic time frames. As is often the case, when they are not rich by the date they had originally planned, they quickly discard the goal. Let's be very clear. It is one thing to set a goal, and quite another to develop an appropriate action plan.

Goals do not entail instant success. Some people expect instant success once they have developed a goal. Just because you know where you want to end up doesn't mean you will not be faced with obstacles, or challenges along the way. Instant success rarely ever happens. You need to be totally dedicated and determined in order to achieve your desired result.

There is no traffic jam on the extra mile.

Dreams and wishes are merely thoughts without concrete action plans. A dream or wish only becomes an attainable goal when it involves taking specific steps. A goal cannot be accomplished without taking concrete action. New Years' Eve is probably not the only time to set a goal. The majority of people, who set goals as part of their New Years' Eve tradition of making resolutions, never seem to accomplish what they intend to.

If you don't design your own life plan, chances are you'll fall into someone else's plan. And guess what they have planned for you? Not much. Goals give you more than a reason to get up in the morning; they are an incentive to keep you going all day. Goals tend to tap the deeper resources and draw the best out of your life. Look to the future, because that is where you'll spend the rest of your life.

There is a very simple seven step process that you can go through to set any goal, whether personal or professional. To be effective, the goal you choose must include all seven of the following steps:

- Identify your goal by writing it down
- Set a deadline for the achievement. Put a date on it.
- List the obstacles to overcome in accomplishing your goal.
- Identify the people and groups you need to work with to reach your goal.
- List the skills and knowledge required to reach your goal. What do you need to know?
- Develop a plan of action to reach your goal.
- Write down the benefits of achieving your goal. (What's in it for me?)

It is important to re-evaluate your goals on a periodic basis to make certain that they are in alignment with what you truly value and want out of life. Remember, goal-setting is a life-long process. Once you have completed one goal, be sure to replace it with something else. This way you will always reap the benefits that goal-setting provides.

Without self-motivation you will not achieve your goals. As the saying goes, "if it's to be it's down to me". Motivational speaker David McNally sets out a number of 'rules' for motivation.

First, your motivation can only come from within yourselves. Why? Because motivation is an internal force that drives individuals to act in order to achieve a specific goal. Two people might read the same book, or listen to the same inspirational speaker but respond differently. One person might feel motivated to act, the other might not.

Second, you must have a big enough 'reason why' in order to feel motivated. Your reason why must provide a 'meaningful motive'. It can be useful to look for a reason that's bigger than yourself. For example, you may want to earn enough money to take care of your family - not just yourself. Dig deep into the truth of what you want. This is why it's so important to choose goals so that you feel a 100% committed.

Third, you need to believe that your goal is attainable. Either that or your fear must be so great that you will try to do it anyway. Without this fear or belief, self-motivation is difficult to maintain. Given that you probably don't want to live with feelings of dread, let's consider belief. You can start by looking for evidence within yourself that proves you can achieve your goal. You can then back this up by seeking support from mentors and role models, either directly or indirectly through books and audios. Anything the mind can conceive and the heart can believe, you can achieve.

Fourth, your environment is an influence on motivation. That's a key reason why you need to choose your friends and colleagues carefully. This doesn't have to mean saying goodbye to the people you know now. But consider whether it would be helpful to make new acquaintances. Again, books and audios can be very supportive when you are looking for new ways of thinking.

Finally, there is a difference between motivation and inspiration. Inspiration is getting in touch with our human spirit, whereas motivation is the driving force to move towards our goal. Inspiration can certainly help self-motivation - and we can look outside ourselves for help with inspiration.

A goal statement is thus an investment in yourself; it clearly identifies what you want, how will you get it, and when will you get it.

Goals must be:

Long term - for 3-5 Years, to provide you with a vision of what you want to do in your lifetime.

Short term - for 6 months to a year to provide you with gratification, to keep you going on a day-to-day basis.

Immediate Goals (milestones leading to ultimate goal) - for 30 Days

Flexible - so you can revise goals as your life changes, as priorities change and as new opportunities arise.

There are two kinds of goals: outcome goals and performance goals which involve actual tasks. **Outcome goal** for a computer course: I am going to get a 3.75 in my computer course this semester. **Performance goal**: I am going to utilize all available lab time, ask my instructor about specific concepts I don't understand and review regularly, not just before quizzes or exams. **Outcome goal** for English: I am going to get at least a B+ on my next paper. **Performance goal**: I am going to improve my English grades by improving my essay writing techniques. I am going to learn to organize my information clearly before I start writing. I am going to proofread my work, finding common mistakes. **Outcome goal** for Math: I am going to earn an 'A' in my math course. **Performance goal**: I am going to improve my grade by studying and working on math problems at least an hour and a half every day. I am going to do all chapter problems, not just the assigned ones. I will work with tutors in the Tutoring Centre whenever needed. If you achieve the tasks in your performance goals, you will achieve your outcome goals.

One question a lot of people ask is how to know if a goal is good or bad. In other words, how do you discriminate between the really important goals and the "nice to have" but not really important ones? You will know whether or not a goal you have chosen is important by answering these five questions.

- Is it really MY goal?
- Is it morally right and fair?
- Are my short-range goals consistent with my long-term goals?

- Can I commit myself emotionally to completing the project?
- Can I visualize myself reaching this goal?

If you have answered "No" to even one of these questions, you may want to reconsider this goal. In the short-term it may appear to work for you, but in the long run, you may end up exposing yourself to a lot of unnecessary conflict and frustration.

Be sure to set big goals as well as multiple goals. Big goals force you to reach in and use the potential that is inside of you. Reach for the sun and, should you miss you will end up amongst the stars. Long-range goals help you to overcome short-range failures. They can also help you to change your direction without going back on your decision. Whether or not they ever reach the goals they have set, people who set big, long- range goals have been found to have higher self-confidence, higher self-esteem, and greater personal motivation. The bottom line is that more than half the rewards and benefits achieved from goal-setting come from actually taking your first step in that direction, regardless of the consequences.

Goal setting requires 100% DISCIPLINE and 100% ATTITUDE:

DISCIPLINE			**ATTITUDE**		
D	=	4	A	=	1
I	=	9	T	=	20
S	=	19	T	=	20
C	=	3	I	=	9
I	=	9	T	=	20
P	=	16	U	=	21
L	=	12	D	=	4
I	=	9	E	=	5
N	=	14			
E	=	5			
		-------			-------
		100			**100**

Turn your Dreams into Reality:

Make sure the goal you are working for is something you really want, not just something that sounds good. It must be consistent with your values. A goal cannot contradict any of your other goals. E.g. you can't buy a Rs.25,00,000 house if your income goal is only Rs.50,000 p.a.

How many seeds are there in an apple? May be five, six, and seven? But how many apples can grow from one seed? Hundreds, thousands, may be more, right? However, the seed has to be in the right place. It should be planted somewhere in the field. It will not sprout if it is kept on a table. Our goal is like a potential seed which will become a full grown tree, provided our goal is also at the right place, like a seed. Which is that right place where you can plant your goals?

Write down your goals in a plain paper. You may have many goals, or few goals. Your goals meet the criteria of specific, measurable, achievable, realistic and time bound, you are maximizing the likelihood that you will achieve them. Take one of the goals that you have listed and develop it against each of the following criteria:

1. Imagine what you really want?
2. Step into it, as though you already have it. Put aside all thoughts of its manifestation. What does this goal look, feel and sound like?
3. Make sure that your goal is within your control. For example, making your child successful in exam is not within your control.
4. Allow yourself to know how achieving the goal takes you one step nearer to achieving a much deeper, longer term goal.
5. Ensure that the achievement of this goal is of real benefit to the key people in your work and in your life.
6. Be clear whether you are willing to pay whatever price necessary to achieve this goal.
7. Decide what your first step towards achieving your plan will be?
8. What is your level of commitment to taking it?
9. Do something today and everyday towards you goal, keeping your eyes on goal.
10. Tap into your creative imagination.
11. Visualize Goals Daily - Your intuition is your direct pipeline to a form of intelligence that is completely beyond your conscious brain. It is accessed by your subconscious mind, which is controlled by the thoughts you think and the beliefs you hold in your conscious mind. The more you affirm and visualize your desired goals in your con-

scious mind, the more readily they are picked up by your subconscious mind and the more rapidly your intuition or creative imagination is triggered. Successful, effective, happy people are those who have latched onto the beam of their own intuitive senses and who rely continuously on their inner guidance. And they seldom make mistakes.

You will often find that your intuition will urge you to either speak up or to remain silent in a social or business situation. Later, that will prove to have been exactly the right thing to do. In retrospect, you will find that your intuitive learning has always been more accurate than anything that you could think of with your conscious mind.

All the truly great writers, composers, artists, and scientists have developed the habit of listening to their intuition. And you have access to the same intuitive powers as the smartest men and women who ever lived.

There is a keen competition at the bottom, but there is always vacancy at the top.

Action Exercises:

Here are three things you can do immediately to put these ideas into action:

First, begin practicing solitude on a regular basis, preferably every day. Sit perfectly still and listen for the voice of intuition to guide you.

Second, follow your intuition, do whatever it tells you. Listen quietly and only do or say what feels perfectly comfortable in every situation.

Third, visualize and affirm your goals regularly. Imagine they are already a reality. This action stimulates your intuition and your creative imagination in wonderful ways. Just try it and see!

3-Steps to Plan your dream:

1. Write your own Personal Mission Statement
2. Break your dreams into many Goals.
3. Write a daily "TO DO" list

DEVELOPING BETTER HABITS

WHAT IS A HABIT?

Habits are routines or behaviours performed regularly and repeatedly. Habits are represented in our brains by collections of neurons, which link together to create a pattern of thinking or behaviour that you fall into automatically. You can think of these collections or clusters as mental maps. They are built gradually over time, and are strengthened by repetition. Habits embed themselves into our daily routine when you make associations.

The quality of your life depends on the quality of your habits. With the same habits, you will end up with the same results, but with better habits, anything is possible. Your life today is essentially the sum of your habits. How in shape or out of shape are you? It is a result of your habits. How happy or unhappy are you? It is a result of your habits. How successful or unsuccessful are you? Again it is a result of your habits.

WHAT IS THE DIFFERENCE BETWEEN SUCCESSFUL AND UNSUCCESSFUL PEOPLE?

When I ask this question in my training sessions, many participants come up with lots of answers like hard work, smart work, clear goals, discipline, and determination. Definitely all these factors play a big role in making you successful. However, what successful people say, and that which I have also experienced in my life is that -

Successful people follow certain Effective Habits, by doing things that Unsuccessful People don't like to do. Successful people instil these effective habits by doing them regularly, deliberately and unnaturally. It's what unsuccessful or average people don't like to do. **So, the difference between successful and unsuccessful people is effective habits.** Your future depends upon your habits. Good habits are hard to form but easy to live with; bad habits are easy to form, but hard to live with. Effective habits can be learned; ineffective habits can be unlearned. It is often wiser to unlearn than to learn. Excellence is an art perfected by training and habituation.

You are what you repeatedly do.
Excellence, then, is not an act, but a habit.

Why do these Extraordinary People develop those Effective habits which they aren't fond of doing? Because by doing those things which they don't like, they achieve what they desire. They have got a purpose in life. They have got a clear cut goal. Clarity of goal gives power. A person with a clear purpose will make progress on even the roughest road. A person with no purpose will make no progress on even the smoothest road.

We don't make our future; we make our habits
and habits make our future.
- APJ Abdul Kalam

POWERFUL FORCES ON DEVELOPING HABITS:

Association:

Neurons that fire together wire together. That is association. When two sets of neurons fire together separately – your 'watching TV' neuron and your 'having your dinner' neuron set for example – links are formed between these two mental maps in your brain. These are not just metaphorical links, they are real, physical connections. When you try to break a habit, it is biology you are fighting, not just psychology.

Repetition:

Repetition is the mother of Habit. The more often you do something, the more it becomes hard-wired into your brains literally. The more often a connection between two neurons fires, the more likely it is to fire again in the future.

HOW TO CREATE A REGULAR PRACTICE HABIT?

Make it easier to repeat by starting tiny things – This is really important. If you make your new habit hard at the beginning, you will run out of steam before you have a chance to get it established. Little hinges swing big doors.

Use association to anchor your habit into your daily routine–Decide carefully when you are going to do your new regular practice habit. Choose a slice of uninterrupted time when you know no one is going to disturb you. Early morning works really well. Now think about something you do every day, without fail, immediately before this bit of time. It might be going for a walk, immediately after reading 10 pages of a book. This act becomes the trigger for your habit, you do your new habit immediately after your trigger. With enough repetition you will build an association and begin to move naturally from your trigger to your habit without thinking.

Take the time to feel good about it – Don't forget this part. Every time you do your new habit, take a moment to congratulate yourself, smile and feel good. When neural connections are accompanied by pleasure, they form much faster and more strongly. Be addicted to a positive habit.

Here are 5 Ways that can help you to break your bad habit:

1. Commitment

Make sure this is something you truly want to accomplish. It's wonderful to "talk the talk," but you'll need to back that up by "walking the walk" as well. Be honest with yourself. Do you truly believe that this is the right time to kick your bad habit? Remember, it has to be done for the right reasons.

Don't let yourself be pressured by others. Search your soul and be certain you're doing this for only one person – you! It's your time and energy you'll be using to make your goal a reality, so make your decision carefully.

2. Start a journal:

Jot down every time you practice your bad habit. This isn't to be used as a punishment, but to give you more of an idea when your undesired behaviour is occurring, so that you can better devise ways to break it.

Include your thoughts and feelings that precede or accompany the behaviour. This can give you an idea if you're doing this when you're under stress, bored, tired, and so on. Though it may seem time consuming at first, recording these thoughts and actions can be a wonderful tools to speed up your success in breaking the habit.

3. Choose an alternative behaviour:

This behaviour can either remind you of your desire to quit or it can be a permanent replacement of your bad behaviour with a desirable one instead. For example, a friend of mine once put a rubber band on her wrist when she wanted to quit smoking. Each time she had the urge to light up a cigarette, she would snap the rubber band on her wrist instead. Naturally, this was only temporary to remind her not to smoke.

Some more ideas are to take a walk, read a book, sing a song, or cook. Any activity can be used as an alternative behaviour. Of course, you don't want to replace one bad habit with another one, but anything that can redirect your focus works well.

4. Start a replacement schedule right away:

Start immediately replacing your bad habit with your alternative, but a gradual shift may work better for you than a complete change. You may want to start with once a week, then maybe twice week, then three times, until you're consistently practicing your alternative behaviour instead of the bad habit.

Remember, this won't happen overnight, so please practice patience. People learn different behaviours at a different pace. Don't be discouraged if your best friend stopped smoking in three weeks and you're on your fifth week and still craving a cigarette.

5. Don't keep this a secret:

If you've made the decision to break a habit, tell others. This is the time when you need the support of your family and friends to help you be successful. Whether you succeed or not, you've taken a major leap in a positive direction. That's why it's so important to share what you hope to accomplish with family and friends. Those who love you will be there to encourage you, offer support, and help you wherever they can.

Breaking a bad habit can be difficult, but it isn't impossible. Use these techniques to make your journey easier, then celebrate your accomplishment when you've succeeded – you deserve it!

When you choose a habit you also choose the end result of that habit.

INSTIGATING HABITS:

These are the life processes you establish to help you in guiding the project of life. These move you towards a chosen idea - Leading to Positivity. They can be enjoyed in their own right without achieving the goal. They steer you on a path that is in itself rewarding. They often have a goal but that is not as important as the movement or the process. These habits are open ended. Because you are not focused on the results, whatever happens can be framed as a success. Examples: Saying good morning to your spouse every morning, going for a walk, reading, spending time with your family,, eating healthy food, improving your skills, etc.

AVOIDING HABITS:

These habits are the ones you try to break like, chewing tobacco, smoking, drinking, gossiping, procrastination, social media addiction along with all other types of addiction. Here you are focused on moving away from something. You repulse the object of the habit. Push it away. Negate. Very result oriented, closed, and restrictive. Either you are in compliance with avoiding or you are not.

To move these habits towards instigating habits — mentally reframe them. For example instead of trying to make stopping being a gossip a habit, make looking for areas in others to compliment as a habit. Done well enough this will naturally crowd out the gossiping and who knows where this will lead.

REGIMENTAL HABITS:

Doing a particular activity the same way each time leaving no room for serendipity. This is a devilish cycle that robs one of being present in the moment. Most people who rile against "habit formation" think of only this kind of habit. Giving control to a regiment is a recipe for a missing life, where you are not being in the present. These habits can become "unconscious" if you don't watch out. Examples: showering, parking in the same place, travelling on the same path, coffee in the morning.

To move these habits towards instigating habits — mentally reframe them. For example when having coffee, really be present. If just for a moment, breath, let the universe in. Sense the flavours, the smells, consider how it came it be in front of you. Who knows where this present moment of awareness will lead to?

UNCONSCIOUS HABITS:

Unfortunately, this is the largest category of habits that operate through you. By their nature you cannot see them. You have to rely on family and friends to help you expose them. Unconscious behaviours that are repeated are the definition of this type of habit. So many of your behaviours you are not consciously in control of and some people have more awareness in this realm than others. These are often the outcomes of your biases. Examples: nail biting speeding, driving too slowly, being negative or a pessimist, etc.

To move these habits towards instigating habits — first they must be discovered. Once exposed, then you can mentally reframe them. For example say you discover that you unconsciously frown in some situations, you have a sour look even though you don't feel sour inside, and it is just a habit formed after months or year of inattention. Now this habit can be reframed as wanting to show happiness. Who knows where this will lead? One thing that has been proven by research is when you smile, you become happier.

TYPES OF HABITS:

There are two types of habits:

- ➢ Automatic
- ➢ Cognitive

Automatic:

Your mind is programmed to create habits. There are many systems and habits that drive your lives. You have the ability to use an automatic response, similar to autopilot on a plane, to complete the majority of the mundane and repetitive situations in your lives. This allows you to get ready in the morning, drive to work, stay up to date on the news, and much more.

An automatic habit is a process that runs independently of an executive order by the person. You might be choking when swallowing a pill, getting nervous when the phone rings, looking down when you have a block, substituting words when you cannot say a word. This process is more or less automatised, and cannot be controlled at all or only with utmost focus, attention and energy. You can force yourself to look into someone's eyes while talking to them, but it will be very hard if you have always looked down. Such habits are really programmed in your brain.

Cognitive:

A cognitive habit is a habitual way of thinking about the same situation without really thinking about it. Examples: I need to make a phone call but I will ask my partner to do it, They want me to speak so I will say no, When I call someone I will stutter, I will never be more fluent, Without my stuttering I would have achieved more. All these habitual thoughts occur without any pressure due to a situation, i.e. 50 people aren't staring at you while you speak or the person on the phone is waiting or you feel a block coming. No, you are under no pressure, but you have pre-conceived lines of thoughts for certain situations.

Cognitive habits are easier to tackle by re-thinking one's constructs. Automatic habits are much more difficult to change.

Make small changes that will change everything.

PERSONALITY DEVELOPMENT

WHAT IS PERSONALITY?

Does personality just mean developing?

- Mere external appearance
- Speech
- Mannerisms
- Behavior in accordance of expectation of a group

No - It is a struggle to march from a lower mind to a higher mind. It is the greatest of all great struggles.

"Personality" is generally defined as a person's reactions and reaction-possibilities to situations faced by them. It is the sum total of behaviour and trends manifested in a person's attempts for social adjustment. It is the name given to one's psychophysical processes and reactions to internal and external stimuli. Thus, only the development of theoretical knowledge does not suffice the definition of personality but it includes the development of practical knowledge - **the knowledge that teaches the art of living.**

Personality is a collection of **emotional, thought** and **behavioural** patterns unique to a person that is consistent over time. The word personality originated from the Latin persona, which means "**mask**".

The dictionary meaning of personality is '**distinctive character**'. Character development and personality integration are almost similar processes but personality is a wider term which includes urges, impulses, motives, tendencies, traits, interests, attitudes, morals etc. whereas the '**character**' is used to denote ethical values and attitudes or a person's self-control. Character is embedded in the total structure of 'personality'. Personality does not consist of any particular quality or group of qualities, but it belongs to the compressed or blended whole of a number of different qualities.

ASPECTS OF PERSONALITY

It involves developing all areas of your life, whether it is physical, mental, intellectual or spiritual. An analysis of present world situations of stress & strain - at individual and society levels show that the loss of values is due to the loss of thorough education for developing an integrated and holistic personality. The present age is therefore the age of personality crises. The more someone is eager to develop an attractive personality, the more they find themselves in the pit of a personality crisis. The urgent need of the hour, therefore, is to impart an education that can give a person an integrated and balanced personality.

In the present system of education, there is immense stress on natural and biological sciences, commerce and economics, computer sciences and applied mathematics, statistics etc. but education in other social sciences and humanities and more particularly, in spiritual subjects is not only relegated to the background but has deliberately been omitted from the curriculum. This has resulted in a great imbalance in development of human personality.

Beauty attracts the eyes,
but personality captures the heart.

HOW TO DEVELOP PERSONALITY?

What helps in the development of personality? In simple terms, Personality development is an initiative to improve certain traits and qualities which contribute to your overall personality. No matter what your age is, there is always a space for improvement. Having a good personality can help you improve your professional and social life.

Let's go to certain important personality development tactics which will help you to understand how to have a better personality:

- **Definitely, it is not just your looks:**

It is not just looks that are important and that define who you are. The personality of an individual is determined by their appearance, behaviour, attitude, education, values and some more varying characteristics. Personality defines who you are and how you respond to various situations. It is essential to focus on personality, which matters the most. However, first impression is last impression and you cannot make a first impression a second time.

- **Dress well:**

Focus on how you dress up for office, party or any other occasion. Wear according to the occasion. Good looks will no doubt add to your personality but what matters the most is how you are dressed up. It plays a major role in personality development.

- **Everybody is unique:**

Remember that each individual is different and has their unique characteristics and qualities. Comparing yourself to others around you only increases your distress, especially when you start focusing on where you are lacking compared to others. It is important that you channelize your energy towards your positive traits. So never imitate anyone; be original. Be the one who you are in reality and never pretend.

Never ever compare yourself with others;
when you do that, you are insulting yourself.

➲ **Awareness of social skills:**

Your etiquettes and manners play a major role in developing your personality. Only good-looks will never be sufficient to take you forward in life or help you in your relationships with people. Instead, hone your social skills. The more success you have in social spheres of your life, the better you will feel about yourself. Try to make use of positive gestures, postures while interacting with others and watch out for your body language too. Interact with different kind of people; never avoid any opportunity to mingle with people. See if your eyes are sweet, you will love people and if your tongue is sweet, people will love you.

Look for opportunities, go to different events, participate in social gatherings and be proactive. The more you eschew social interaction, the worse you will feel about yourself. I would suggest you be gregarious. This is also one of the more promising personality development tips.

➲ **Your biggest enemy is your Comfort Zone:**

Be in effort zone rather than in comfort zone. Be prepared to challenge yourself by learning new skills. When you challenge yourself you become unchallenging. For most people it is a huge learning curve to start an online business, so you must have a very positive, open-minded attitude and embrace any changes you need to make.

➲ **Face the Fear:**

Show a single person who have succeeded without making any mistakes. Don't worry about making mistakes, you will make loads in your journey and a lot of them may hold you back for a while, but once you have made them, those mistakes can be eliminated and you can move on.

➲ **Popularise yourself in a positive way:**

Show the world you are alive in true spirit. Build your Brand and show yourself in all your communications. Whatever content you put out there is a slice of your personality, so make sure it shows you in a positive light. It is you that you are trying to sell to other people, so the more personal the message the better.

➲ **Come Across As A Leader:**

Whatever you learn and however little you know, use it well. Become an authority on whatever topic you tackle, then you will have the knowledge to pass it on to others and if you put your message across in the right way, you will attract followers. Express yourself and always do what you say.

➲ **Never Ever Give Up:**

Change the old wisdom – DO or DIE to DO BEFORE YOU DIE. I know this sounds like an obvious one to end on, but there are loads of people who literally could have made it through with only a few more weeks or months of effort. They had done everything right apart from seeing it through to success and it was just that final bit of belief that prevented them.

NEVER EVER GIVE UP

➲ **Be humorous and don't be serious all the time:**

No one likes to be with boring and serious people. Everyone enjoys the company of someone who makes them laugh. Laughter is a therapy. Do not beat around the bush just to make others laugh. Try to add fun while having the conversation; others will naturally be attracted to you.

Some more good personality development tips at a glance:

- Keep a smart head and keep cool.
- Don't Copy anyone.
- Create your own personal style
- Don't doubt yourself
- Be An Active Listener
- Learn to have patience and focus on your communication skills. Be polite and gentle with your words.
- Be executive in dressing
- Don't shout or be aggressive.
- Be more passionate about your work and be optimistic.
- Accept And Recognize Your Weak Points
- Learn to appreciate others. It helps the same qualities to grow in you too.

Personality is a mask you believe it

SELF-ESTEEM

WHAT IS SELF-IMAGE?

How you look at yourself is more important than how others look at you. Self-image is yet another one of the **"self" concepts** essential to understand in positive psychology. Although related to the others, it is a distinct concept that has its own place and its own importance. As you might imagine, self-image is related to what you see when you look in a mirror—however, it goes much deeper than that. Self-image refers to how we see ourselves on a more global level, both internally and externally.

Self-image can be defined as your appreciation of your own worth and importance. It is having the character to be accountable for your own behavior and acting responsibly toward others.

WHAT IS SELF-ESTEEM?

Self-esteem refers to a person's overall sense of their value or worth. It can be considered a sort of measure of how much a person "values, approves of, appreciates, prizes, or likes themselves". Self-esteem is quite simply one's attitude toward oneself and can be described as a "favourable or unfavourable attitude toward the self".

Various factors believed to influence our self-esteem include:

- Genetics
- Personality
- Life experiences
- Age
- Health
- Thoughts
- Social circumstances
- The reactions of others
- Comparing yourself to others

An important note is that self-esteem is not fixed. It is malleable and measurable, meaning we can test for and improve upon it.

DIFFERENCE BETWEEN SELF-IMAGE AND SELF-ESTEEM:

Similarly, self-image has a lot to do with self-esteem. After all, how we see ourselves is a big contributing factor to how we feel about ourselves.

However, self-esteem goes deeper than self-image. Self-esteem is the overall sense of respect for ourselves and involves how favourably (or unfavourably) we feel about ourselves.

Having a negative self-image can certainly influence self-esteem, and having low self-esteem is likely to be accompanied by a negative self-image, but they are at least somewhat independent "self" aspects.

HOW SELF-ESTEEM DEVELOPS?

- During childhood, from your earliest experiences and feedback about you. In adolescence, by comparing yourself to others on:
    - Physical appearance
    - Body image

TIPS FOR IMPROVING YOUR SELF-ESTEEM:

1. Identify and Challenge Your Negative Beliefs:

The first step is to identify, and then challenge, your negative beliefs about yourself. Notice your thoughts about yourself. For example, you might find yourself thinking 'I am not clever enough to do that' or 'I have no friends'. When you do, look for evidence that contradicts those statements. Write down both statement and evidence, and keep looking back at it to remind yourself that your negative beliefs about yourself are not true.

2. Identify the Positive About Yourself:

It is also a good idea to write down positive things about yourself, such as being good at a sport, or nice things that people have said about you. When you start to feel low, look back at these things, and remind yourself that there is plenty of good about you. In general, positive internal dialogue is a big part of improving your self-esteem. If you catch yourself saying things like 'I'm not good enough' or 'I'm a failure', you can start to turn things around by saying 'I can beat this' and 'I can become more confident by viewing myself in a more positive way. In the beginning you will catch yourself falling back into old negative habits, but with regular effort you can start to feel more positive and build your self-esteem as well. A man lost everything in fire and next day he placed a sign board – shop burnt goods burnt, but luckily no damage to faith and confidence. The shop will start tomorrow. Success is like a train; it has several compartments – hard work, focus, luck etc. but leading all those compartments is the engine of self-confidence. So be self-confident and enthusiastic.

3. Build Positive Relationships-and Avoid Negative Ones:

You will probably find that there are certain people-and certain relationships-that make you feel better than others. If there are people who make you feel bad about yourself, try to avoid them. Build relationships with people who make you feel good about yourself and avoid the relationships that drag you down.

4. Give Yourself a Break:

You don't have to be perfect every hour of every day. You don't even have to feel good about yourself all the time. Self-esteem varies from situation to situation, from day to day and hour to hour. Some people feel relaxed and positive with friends and colleagues, but uneasy and shy with strangers. Others may feel totally in command of themselves at work but struggle socially (or vice versa). Give yourself a break. We all have times when we feel a bit down or find it harder to maintain our self-belief. The key is not to be too hard on yourself. Be kind to yourself, and not too critical. Avoid criticising yourself to others, because this can reinforce your negative views—and also give other people a (possibly false) negative opinion of you. You can help to boost your self-esteem by giving yourself a treat whenever you succeed in doing something hard, or just for managing a particularly bad day.

5. Become More Assertive and Learn to Say No:

People with low self-esteem often find it hard to stand up for themselves or to say no to others. This means that they may become overburdened at home or at work, because they do not like to refuse anyone anything. However, this can increase stress, and make it even harder to manage. Developing your assertiveness can therefore help to improve your self-esteem. Sometimes acting as if you believe in yourself can actually help to increase self-belief!

6. Improve your physical health:

It is much easier to feel good about ourselves when we are fit and healthy. However, people with low self-esteem often neglect themselves, because they do not feel that they 'deserve' to be looked after. Try taking more exercise, eating well, and getting enough sleep. It is also a good idea to make time to relax and to do something that you want to do, rather than something that someone else expects you to do. You may find that simple changes like this can make a huge difference to your overall outlook. Relax! Even your wife shouts at you.

7. Take on Challenges:

People with low self-esteem often avoid challenging and difficult situations. One way to improve your self-esteem can actually be to take on a challenge. This doesn't mean that you need to do everything yourself—part of the challenge might be to seek help when you need it—but be prepared to try something that you know will be difficult to achieve. By succeeding, you show yourself that you can achieve your goals. This challenges your negative beliefs and will therefore improve your self-esteem.

Low self-esteem cycle:

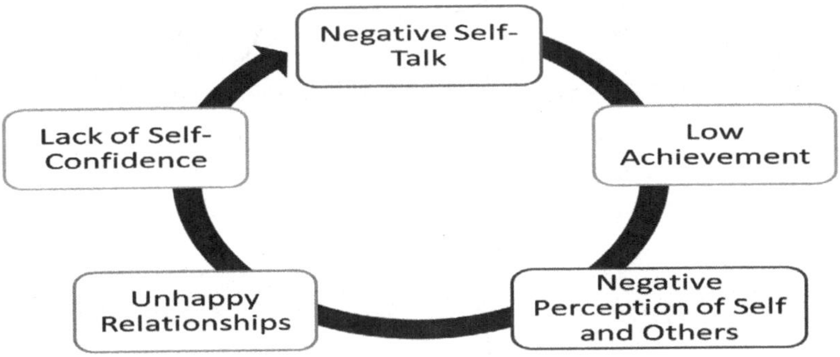

High Self-esteem cycle:

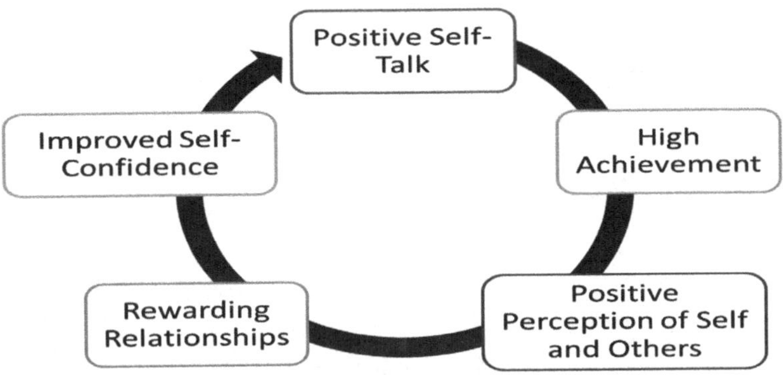

Enhanced Self-Esteem cycle:

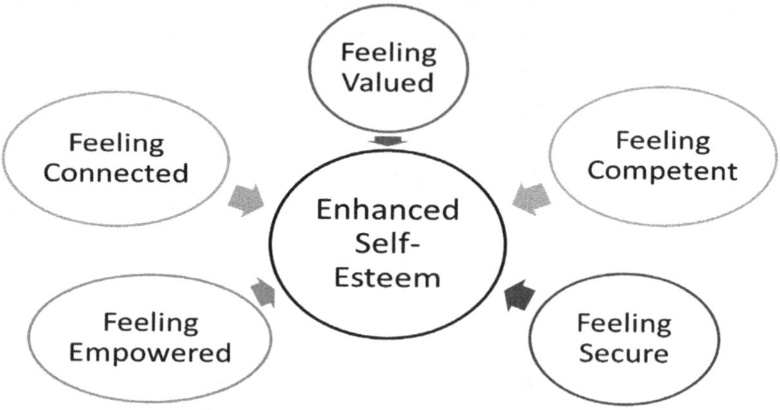

THE END

Send your feebacks to
maxlivemediasolutions@gmail.com
jkvital@gmail.com